Princely Chandos

James Brydges 1674–1744

James Brydges

Princely Chandos

James Brydges 1674–1744

Joan Johnson

ALAN SUTTON
1984

Alan Sutton Publishing Limited
17a Brunswick Road
Gloucester

First published 1984

Copyright © 1984 Joan Johnson

All rights reserved. No part of this publication may be
reproduced, stored in a retrieval system, or transmitted,
in any form or by any means, electronic, mechanical photocopying,
recording or otherwise, without the prior permission of the
publishers and copyright holder.

British Library Cataloguing in Publication Data

Johnson, Joan, *1915–*
   Princely Chandos.
   1. Chandos, James Brydges, *Duke of*
   2. Great Britain—Nobility—Biography
   I. Title
   942.06'6'0924   DA483.C5

ISBN 0-86299-115-3

Typesetting and origination by
Alan Sutton Publishing Limited.
Photoset Baskerville 10.5/12
Printed in Great Britain

Contents

Illustrations		6
Introduction		9
Chapter 1	Family Background and Early Years	14
Chapter 2	Political Commitments: 1698–1719	32
Chapter 3	Business Associates and Family Life	53
Chapter 4	London Life and Friends	68
Chapter 5	Family Responsibilities	82
Chapter 6	New Interests and Diversions	101
Chapter 7	Chandos and his Fellow Builders	119
Chapter 8	Management of Estates and Gardens	140
Chapter 9	The 1730's and After	155
Epilogue		170
Notes		183
Bibliography		186
Acknowledgments		188
Index		189

Illustrations

James Brydges. Dahl. Courtauld Institute.	2
Dr Busby of Westminster. Artist unknown. National Portrait Gallery.	19
Old Palace Yard, Westminster. Kip engraving. British Museum.	20
Garden Quadrangle, New College. Burghers 1729. The Hope Collection, Ashmolean Museum.	23
Wrought Iron Gates, New College. Photo: Anthony Kersting.	24
Mary Lake and her son. Hudson. Private Collection.	27
Red Lion Square. 18th Century print. Private Collection.	29
Golden Square. 18th Century print. Private Collection.	30
Prince George of Denmark. attrib. Riley. National Portrait Gallery.	34
Henry St John, Viscount Bolingbroke. attrib. Richardson. National Portrait Gallery.	37
Sir Robert Walpole. Kneller 1710. National Portrait Gallery.	38
The Duke of Marlborough. Closterman 1700. Private Collection.	43
The Duchess of Marlborough. Kneller 1700. Private Collection.	44
Robert Harley, Earl of Oxford. Kneller 1714. National Portrait Gallery.	46
The Palace of St James's. Sayers. The Hope Collection, Ashmolean Museum.	49
James Brydges, 1st Duke of Chandos. Dahl 1719. Courtauld Institute.	50
Sir Josiah Child. Riley. Courtauld Institute.	55
Sir Hans Sloane. Slaughter 1736. National Portrait Gallery.	56
The Drummond Family. Zoffany. Yale Centre for British Art. Paul Mellon Collection	59
Cassandra Willoughby, 1st Duchess of Chandos. after Kneller. Collection of Lord Middleton.	63
St James's Square. Sutton Nicholls 1727. Private Collection.	69
Ranelagh Gardens. Universal Magazine. The Hope Collection, Ashmolean Museum.	79

Illustrations

Conversation Piece at Wanstead. Nollekens 1740. Yale Center for British Art. Paul Mellon Collection.	80
The Hon. Mary Leigh. Kersebloom. Courtauld Institute.	89
Brereton Bourchier. Verelst. Private Collection.	90
George Frederick Handel. Hudson 1756. National Portrait Gallery.	97
York Buildings and the Water Works. 18th Century print. The Hope Collection, Ashmolean Museum.	103
Shaw Hall, Newbury. Newbury Museum.	107
The Bath House, Tunbridge Wells. Private Collection.	109
The Pantiles, Tunbridge Wells. British Museum.	110
The Road to Bath. Malton. The Hope Collection, Ashmolean Museum.	113
Wanstead House. Metz. Guildhall Library.	117
The Town House of Ralph Allen. Courtauld Institute.	123
Prior Park, Bath. Walker 1750. Private Collection.	124
Dyrham Park. Photo: Anthony Kersting.	128
Ditchley Park. Private Collection.	131
The Hall, Ditchley. Photo: Anthony Kersting.	132
The Stoning of St Stephen. Carving: Grinling Gibbons.	134
Cirencester House and Park. Photo: Anthony Kersting.	149
Canons: Stone Perch. Photo: Country Life Magazine.	151
Canons: Garden Urn. Photo: Country Life Magazine.	152
Lydia, Lady Davall, 2nd Duchess of Chandos. Hudson. Courtauld Institute.	159
Anne Jefferies, 3rd Duchess of Chandos. Highmore. Walker Art Gallery.	160
Lady Jane and Lady Catherine Brydges. Hudson. Private Collection.	163
Lord Wilton. Devis. Courtauld Institute.	164
The Grounds at Wanstead. Kayff. Private Collection.	169
Canons rebuilt. Private Collection.	173
Interior of Great Witley Church. National Monument Record.	174
St Lawrence's Church, Whitchurch. Photo: Anthony Kersting.	181

THE BRYDGES FAMILY

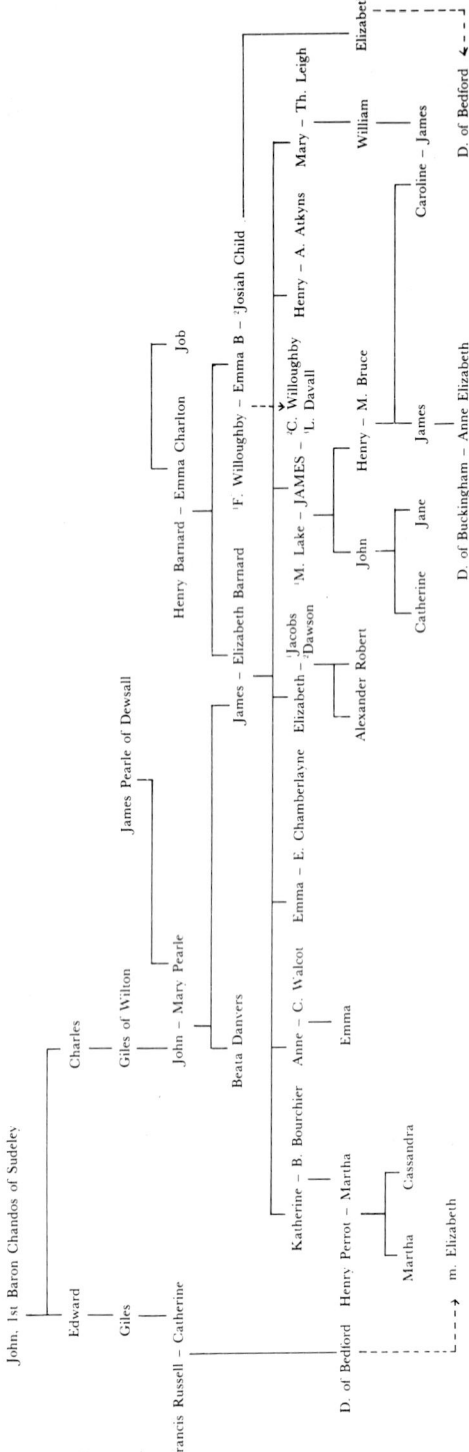

Introduction

James Brydges (1674–1744) later to become the first Duke of Chandos, the 'Princely Chandos', lived during a period of transition, a time of preparation for the great changes that were to revolutionise government and society in Britain during the later 18th century and 19th century.

Constitutionally, the country moved from the near absolutism of Charles II to a situation under the first Hanoverian monarchs, where the King's power was largely subordinated to that of politicians able to command votes both inside and outside Parliament. Economically, commercial enterprise began to dominate the scene, bringing about an expansion of domestic and overseas trade and thus of ports and markets, and changing fundamentally the customary basis of life for the majority of the population. For some while yet, directly or indirectly, agriculture was to remain the chief means of subsistence of a large number of people, but the application of capital and adoption of a commercial approach to landowning and land usage, gradually turned this into as much a business proposition as any transaction carried out on the Royal Exchange.

Members of the landed classes still enjoyed great privileges; they also shouldered the heaviest responsibilities where the payment of taxes, holding of governmental office and maintenance of law and order were concerned; but political power was gradually passing into the hands of those who had money as opposed to estates, and with it the importance of local persons and centres of influence. For the moneyed people were merchants, bankers and speculators – mainly based in London and in a position to influence governmental policy; and as national considerations came to supersede provincial ones, so the importance of the capital increased, not only as the centre of government and the nation's trade, but also as the source of social and aesthetic trends, because wealth was a prerequisite of patronage. Such times of change were generally unsettling, although they afforded opportunities for anyone inclined to take advantage of them. However, of those who aimed not merely to survive but also to succeed, confidence, resilience and endless versatility were demanded. James Brydges was a man fired with contemporary interests and enthusiasm, qualified in many ways to be an outstanding figure in his own time and to establish a lasting reputation for himself; yet his achievements fell short of this promise.

Although never considered a leading figure in politics, Brydges as a young man certainly aspired to become one. In London during the 1690's, he assiduously courted important people 'whose assistance hereafter may be very beneficiall' and thus established contacts with the court of William III and with Princess Anne and her husband: while during a tour abroad between 1692 and 1694 he cultivated friends and acquaintances at the Electoral court of Hanover who were to stand him in good stead when a Hanoverian succeeded to the English throne in 1714. His association with the Marlboroughs necessarily brought him into prominence during the years of their ascendancy, but surprisingly did not diminish his prestige when the Duke was discredited by his political opponents and the Duchess quarrelled with Queen Anne and lost her position at court.

However, after the achievement of his dukedom in 1719 'in recognition of his having given the first years of his adult life to the State', Brydges's political ambitions were halted and his activities largely limited to the acquisition of lucrative sinecures for himself and the manipulation of borough elections on behalf of his sons. He seems to have revelled in the reputation of having influence and therefore being approached and asked for favours of various kinds, while becoming extremely irritated at times with the large number of importunate requests that he received. One of the duties of his second wife Cassandra was to deal with these and by means of carefully worded letters, excuse his Lordship from conceding any favours, at the same time concealing whether, in fact, he was in a position to do so anyway.

Brydges played a part in the politics of his time from the sidelines. He was much more fully committed to the contemporary world of business. One of his first adventures while a young boy had been a journey with his family to Constantinople where his father had an appointment as an agent of the Turkey company and an ambassador for England. His maternal grandfather, Sir Henry Barnard, was a Turkey merchant; his aunt Emma Barnard, who was to become his mother-in-law also, had as her second husband Sir Josiah Child, a governor of the East India Company; his sister Elizabeth married another Turkey merchant, Alexander Jacob; so inevitably in the family circle, trade must have been a frequent topic of conversation. But inclination also drew Brydges into the company of those who were taking advantage of the opportunities of the time to promote business ventures and financial speculations. He joined the clubs and frequented the coffee-houses where the latest news could be heard and useful contacts made; and always his propensity for gambling and his credulity led him into committing himself to any promising or even unpromising proposition. 'He was a bubble to every project and a dupe to men that nobody else almost would keep company with'. His interests and speculations embraced every aspect of contemporary exploration and expansion – land development, building, water supplies and transport, overseas trade, manufacture – and frequent failures did nothing to deter him from taking further risks.

Much though he enjoyed his sorties into the world of business, Brydges felt even more strongly the urge to emulate his contemporaries in the pursuit of a way of life fitted to his circumstances. The possession of estates, the achievement of public office, the acquisition of wealth and promotion to dukedom – all these were factors which in his estimation demanded sound domestic economy, residences up to date in their architecture and furnishings, entertainment on a sumptuous scale, and a generous bestowal of patronage. He lived through a period of considerable changes in taste and values that corresponded roughly with contemporary political developments. The relaxed atmosphere ushered in by the Restoration led to a liking for and indulgence in Baroque architecture and extravagant fashions in dress; French and later Dutch influences introduced new styles in furnishings and in the lay-out of gardens; and after the accession of the Hanoverians and the decline of the royal court as a cultural force, members of the aristocracy imbued with the effects of a classical education and the Grand Tour of Europe, determined the standards of those aspiring to be arbiters of taste.

It was the earliest of these influences that most appealed to Brydges, and led to a flamboyance in his style of living and behaviour that inspired unfavourable criticism even when he was at the height of his fame, and later was to be deplored by the upholders of classical asceticism. The ascendancy of the Baroque was short-lived and had only limited appeal anyway, but there is no doubt that for a while the splendour of Canons (Brydges's out-of-town house at Edgware) and the grandeur of the parish church of St. Lawrence at Whitchurch which he had rebuilt at his own expense, epitomised what the Baroque enthusiasts were striving after; just as the architects, artists, musicians and gardeners he employed, were those most skilled in achieving approved effects and therefore most in demand in fashionable circles.

Almost inseparable from his aristocratic role as an exponent of fashionable trends were his responsibilities as a landowner, which Brydges took very seriously. Like many of his contemporaries, he believed that it was not enough to regard estates as a mere means of subsistence; they must, if possible, be made to yield profits that could be ploughed back to secure improvements, so that ultimately the land that had been inherited or acquired was in better heart and more productive than before: and anyone who worked or was dependent on it, would likewise be better off.

However, behind Brydges the puller of political strings, the business entrepreneur, conscientious landlord and ducal patron, there was a more private person, regarded with affection by his family and with genuine gratitude by the many people whom he befriended and helped. He never inspired the awe that perhaps he hoped for, to judge by the senatorial pose he chose for the portrait painted by Dahl and his monument in the church at Whitchurch; and he was acutely sensitive to the criticism and ridicule sometimes levelled at him. The splendour and panache of his public appearances disguised an underlying lack of confidence that could make him behave stubbornly and foolishly on occasion; and although he was a great collector of books throughout his life and had a magnificent library at Canons, he was not particularly intellectual. For music he had a genuine fondness; he was a competent flute-player, appreciated the company of friends who could perform, or listen to other players with him; and while making it contribute to his public image, he also cherished his company of musicians at Canons as a source of personal and private pleasure.

Brydges's relations with his two sons were somewhat uneasy, since both were headstrong and temperamental, and he was inclined to be inconsistent in his dealings with them, alternating indulgence with dictatorial authority. On the other hand, each of his three wives in turn loved him, bore patiently with his foibles, boosted his morale when necessary, and in the case of the second, Cassandra, willingly performed the services of a secretary, personal assistant and public relations officer rolled into one. His nephews, nieces and grandchildren, as well as numerous godchildren enjoyed visits to Canons and were conscious of his kindness and good intentions for them. And there is no doubt that in order to sustain his role as Duke of Chandos, owner of vast estates and controller of the lives of numerous dependants, he needed the quiet times spent in the heart of his family, playing cards, looking at his pictures and books, listening to music, and relieved of the need to be anxious about the impression he was making on other people.

A legend in his own time, Brydges provoked extreme reactions – admiration or scorn, eulogies or satire. Subsequently, the details of his career have tended to be forgotten, and only the recorded magnificence of Canons or the performance of one of the Chandos anthems recalls the man without whom none of these things would have come into existence. Yet in the course of his career, he had dealings with so many people, was a party to such varied undertakings, and brought together in his service men with such a wide range of skills, that he was very much a part of contemporary history, and typical of his class, upbringing and background. His life was full and varied since he made the most of his time and opportunities, whether in London, on his estates in the country, or at the fashionable resorts of Tunbridge Wells and Bath. His great wealth and the comfort and pleasure it secured for him can indeed be contrasted unfavourably with the growing poverty of the lower classes at the time. Alexander Pope was particularly scathing about 'such lavish cost and little skill', and only cynically conceded that men like the princely Chandos did some good by providing employment: 'hence the poor are clothed, the hungry fed'.

But it would be unfair to condemn Brydges for not being more enlightened than his contemporaries. He was essentially a product of the age he lived in and had neither the confidence nor the convictions to do other than accept the values of his time. A few may have suffered as a result of his sins of omission or commission, but many had reason to be grateful for his kindness and generosity, and in particular all those who came within the framework of his 'family' (i.e. his relatives, friends and dependants) justly regarded him with respect and affection.

CHAPTER 1

Family Background And Early Years

The Brydges family was a large and affectionate one. James Brydges, eighth Lord Chandos and his wife Elizabeth cared deeply for their children, considering their interests and needs, and doing their best to give the boys a useful education and to find suitable husbands for the girls. They frequently had nephews, nieces and grandchildren to stay, and included them in the affection and approval they gave to their own children. A letter written by grandson William Leigh (aged 9) to his parents, while staying with the Brydges, opened with greetings to his parents, touched briefly on what he and his brothers were doing and then dried up:

> My grandmother won't tell me what to write and I don't know what to write: and since your lordship have me write, you must ene take it as it is.

and this was endorsed with great pride by Lord Chandos:

> I made your son write this in the room by me because I would be sure nobody should help him, and I think its pretty for the first letter from such a child as he is.

James Brydges the younger had two brothers and five sisters in whom – even during his parents' lifetime – he took a caring interest, and whose well-being he assumed as his responsibility after his father's death in 1714, although by then they were all grown up. This concern was recognised by his mother who wrote in her will (dated 1717) 'I die, my dear children and grandchildren, in very poor circumstances, but you have a good brother', and this indeed proved to be the case since both his brothers gained preferment through his good offices, and two of his sisters – who remained a source of worry to him even after marriage – were continually in receipt of money and moral support, family feeling proving stronger than any personal irritation or impatience they may

Family Background and Early Years

have roused in him.

James was born on January 6th 1674 at the home of his father's parents, Dewsall in Herefordshire. His arrival was greeted with delight, since his mother had already had and lost several children and James was the first son to survive. He then spent his early years in the company and homes of relatives and friends, all of whom were gentry, with interests primarily but not exclusively in the land. His father was descended from the old family of Chandos, members of which had served their kings as soldiers and administrators and been rewarded with estates in the counties of Hereford, Worcester and Gloucester. These they had consolidated and added to by purchases and advantageous marriages until they had very considerable holdings in these areas and in Radnorshire as well. James's grandfather, Sir John Brydges, owned estates round Wilton Castle, Hereford, and his grandmother was the heiress to lands belonging to the Pearle family at Dewsall and Aconbury in the same county.[1] James's mother Elizabeth was the daughter and co-heiress of Sir Henry Barnard, a Shropshire gentleman who combined landowning with the successful handling of business. The first husband of his aunt Emma Barnard was Francis Willoughby, the eminent naturalist and owner of estates in Warwickshire and Nottinghamshire; while his maternal grandmother was a Charlton, sister of Sir Job who lived at Ludford, Shropshire and had estates in the neighbourhood of Ludlow. There was also a cousin relationship between the Brydges and the Russells of Woburn, and the Scudamores of Kentchurch. Thus through the West Midlands stretched a network of related families with similar interests and ambitions, members of which visited and corresponded with each other, supported each other in various ways, and promoted further marriages that would safeguard their lines and estates.

At the time of James's birth, the lands of his own family and those with whom he had ties of kinship, were situated in areas that were still largely agricultural. The Willoughbys did have coal on their Nottinghamshire estates and owed part of their wealth to this, but the Brydges, Charltons and Barnards used their land or leased it to others for agricultural purposes. These Welsh border counties were rich and profitable, with good pasture in the river valleys supporting dairy cattle: orchards producing fruit (much of it used for cider and perry) and incidentally providing sustenance for pigs: arable land bearing crops of wheat and barley: and in Gloucestershire especially, hill grazing for sheep. Woodland and copses afforded game, and the rivers salmon and other fresh fish. Thus families like the Brydges were able to be self-sufficient in bare

These are to congratulate my dear Brother and
Sister safe journey into the country, and to assure you
that none can be better satisfied in the marriage
of a sister, than I am in my dear Sisters happy settlement with you, a person of that temper and
humour, that I am certain, (when time renders me
capable of enjoying) I shall think my self very happy
in the yo[u]r conversation. I know your spare minutes
are better employed, than to admit of any correspondence
with a school boy, neither can I expect you should indulge me with so great a favour, in the capacity
now am in. This is only to assure you that my hearty
prayers and wishes are for the happyness and prosperity
of your selfe and my dear sister, and that you shall
always finde me not only a Brother in my best affections,
between us, but a servant to you both as long as I live.
God almighty preserve you both, and send you long
life, to enjoy one another; and if I live I question not
but I shall be happy in you both, for I aim at nothing
but a true cordiall affection between us, that wee may
always live and love as Brothers, and pray you both to
beleive that the first oppertunity I can lay hold of, shall
demonstrate that I really am

Old palace yard   Dear Brother & Sister
Decemb: 12: 1689:   your most affection: Broth:
Pray accept my hearty   & humble Servant
and true affections your selfe,
& give the same to my Sisters,   James Brydges
& make hast up againe for your
companys are very much missed
just now by me.

Family Background and Early Years

necessities. Since the 16th century however, they were by no means content to derive a mere subsistence from their lands. With expanding markets close at hand, also further afield in the Midlands and London, and experimental new methods being mooted that promised to increase the yield of crops and improve the quality of livestock, the Brydges were among those who prepared the way for greater changes in the 18th century, by trying out new crops, draining and fertilising their arable land, and specialising in the cattle and sheep they kept.

However, although the status and success of the Brydges and their friends was derived from being estate owners, they were by no means narrow or circumscribed in their attitudes and interests. As early as the 16th century many landed gentlemen, while following progressive policies in respect of their estates, were aware that if they were to advance their fortunes substantially, they needed additional sources of income. Thus some sought paid positions, some acquired business interests, some speculated with any money they could spare. The law – Sir Job Charlton trained at Lincoln's Inn and was Chief Justice of Chester: government office – the eighth Lord Chandos was an ambassador: participation in the great trade companies – Sir Henry Barnard was a member of the Turkey Company: could all provide financial returns which facilitated a rising standard of living and the injection of capital into estates for the purpose of improvement; and it seems unlikely that the Brydges, the Charltons and the Barnards for instance, would have been equally at home on their estates and in London, and in a position to assume public responsibilities, had it not been for the financial means, useful contacts and experience they acquired from their wider interests and commitments.

Traditionally the Brydges were royalist in their sympathies, and until the 17th century, their loyalty had brought its own rewards in the shape of titles, lands, royal appointments and ultimately the position of Lord Lieutenant of Gloucestershire and the wardenship of Sudeley Castle. But during the Civil Wars their fortunes had been reversed. Lord George Chandos, unwisely trying to raise troops for the King in Cirencester, narrowly escaped being torn to pieces, and subsequently after a struggle to retain Sudeley as a Royalist stronghold, was obliged to flee; and in spite of changing sides in an attempt to preserve his estates, lost these and his reputation at the same time.[2] Similar sufferings befell the Charltons who sold much of their property in order to be able to lend money to the King, and to the Willoughby family whose home at Nottingham was occupied by Parliamentary troops for the duration of the war and badly damaged.

The loyalty of all these families to the monarchy was bound up with a matching loyalty to the established church. Family prayers and regular attendance at services were part of the routine of their daily lives; also, like other landed gentry, they either had powers of patronage or friends with the same, so that possible openings could be found in the church for members of the family. James's younger brother Henry for instance was helped into the living of Broadwell, Gloucestershire by Theophilus Leigh, James's brother-in-law, whose preferment it was. Even without such vested interests, it would have been instinctive for them to consider their political and religious loyalties inseparable; but this way of thinking created a problem when James II, himself a Roman Catholic, attempted to re-establish Catholicism in England against the terms of his coronation oath and the wishes of the majority of his subjects. The eighth Lord Chandos, who had shown a certain capacity for 'Trimming' in 1679–80 when his appointment as ambassador was in the balance,[3] now had definite reservations about opposing his anointed sovereign as did his relatives the Leighs, and until his death he, like them, continued to hold Jacobite sympathies, thus causing Burnet to comment: 'He was warm against King William's reign and doth not make any great figure in this' (Queen Anne's).

Meanwhile his son, avowing similar loyalties to the twin pillars of the Establishment, was trying to persuade him that it might be wiser to go along with the trend of events that was carrying England in the direction of the Hanoverian succession. For young James Brydges, although surrounded by examples of consistency and integrity during his early years, was later much more influenced by the politicians and business men he had dealings with, and it was no doubt from them that he learned the uses of expediency and the importance of being able to shift one's ground according to circumstances, in order to survive worldly vicissitudes. It was this side of his character that inspired Swift's description of him: 'A very worthy gentleman, but a great complier with every court.'

James's childhood was typically that of a boy of his class. The Brydges were comfortably off, but the needs and commitments of such a large family were considerable, and this fact coupled with a streak of meanness in James Brydges senior, meant that they never lived luxuriously. Whether actually occupied or not, several family houses – namely Wilton, Aconbury, Dewsall, together with a base in London, had to be kept ready for use with a skeleton staff in residence; and when the family moved from one to another, servants went with them and supplies and some furniture also. For instance, before sending some of her children to

Dr Busby of Westminster School

Old Palace Yard, Westminster

stay with the Leighs at Adlestrop, Lady Chandos wrote:

> I will be shure to send the field-bed ... I will also send 2 sets of curtains and beding according to your desire, but I have not one press bed in the house, but if anything else that we have maybe of use by the return of our coach, pray let me know it.[4]

From an early age the children were accustomed to being sent to stay with relatives while their mother produced yet another addition to their family (she had 22 children in all) and these visits encouraged in them an independence and self-reliance that was a useful preparation for life. They also afforded contacts that led to marriage. James's sister Anne met her future husband Charles Walcot through the Charltons, and Elizabeth hers – Alexander Jacob – through the Barnards. At the Barnards and the Charltons also James himself got to know his cousin Cassandra Willoughby, later to become his second wife, and made the acquaintance of her step-father Sir Josiah Child, whose son Richard in due course was to embark on the rebuilding of Wanstead House while James was refashioning and refurbishing his own house at Canons.

Elizabeth Brydges, James's mother, would have undertaken the training of her daughters in domestic skills – the ordering of household supplies, the management of servants, needlework and the making of cordials and simple medicines; and they seem also to have had some formal teaching since all proved to be quite fluent and literate writers later on. It is not certain how much education her son James had had when he departed with her for Constantinople in 1680, but since the household there would have had a resident chaplain James and his younger brothers Henry and Francis may have been taught by him. Certainly on their return in 1686 they were all sent to Westminster School which presupposes some preparation, since at the time this was one of the best educational establishments in the country. Under the direction of Dr. Busby, Headmaster for nearly 50 years, strict discipline and good scholarship prevailed there, and although the curriculum was narrowly classical, the tutors really did try to instil some academic values into their pupils, of whom many proceeded to Oxford, Cambridge and the Inns of Court. Lord Chandos's anxiety to get the boys accepted at Westminster and under the eagle eye of Dr. Busby is reflected in the letter he sent along with them from Constantinople, recommending:

> these poor little boys, for they all three of them being of age and competent, natural and acquired also capacities to partake of the

benefit of your (throughout the whole learned world) most famous and incompatable methods in teaching. I have thought it a sin . . . to venture the loss of time for their preferment to the honour and inescapable advantage of being adopted to the number of your scholars; and although at present they are not worthy the form immediately under your care and conduct, yet I am in good hopes their diligence and painstaking (by vertue of Dr. Knipe's helping hand) will in a short space raise them to it.[5]

While the boys were at Westminster, their father leased a house in Old Palace Yard, not far from the school and convenient for his own political activities at court after his return from Constantinople. This the family continued to use as their base until Lord Chandos retired from active politics after the accession of William III and the young James went up to Oxford to finish his academic education at New College.

Oxford at this time was a stronghold of Jacobite and High Church sentiments. The sufferings of the city and the University as a result of supporting Charles I during the Civil Wars had served to strengthen their royalist sympathies; thus while continuing to hold their positions under William III, University officials and heads of colleges reserved their loyalty to the Stuarts. Another sign of the times was the widespread rebuilding that was going on. As circumstances became more prosperous and more stable, University and college buildings were improved and extended, and in the case of the latter, more residential accommodation provided, and grounds and gardens laid out. Then, as now, present and past students were asked to contribute to expenses, and in 1710, some years after he had gone down, James Brydges gave £100 towards the cost of the Garden Quadrangle at New College, 'a building lately raised for Noblemen and Gentlemen Commoners.'[6] Though careful with his money, Lord Chandos would not have wanted his son to present a poor appearance or to live in circumstances unbecoming a Gentleman Commoner, so James would have had at least one servant, a groom, his own horses and an allowance to meet expenses over and above the tutor's fees, board and lodging, books and customary dues paid by his father.

It is difficult to decide to what extent Brydges was genuinely academic in his inclinations and ability. He came down from Oxford at the end of two years in 1692, without taking a degree, as was quite customary for anyone not needing a qualification for proceeding into the church or the legal profession; nevertheless it was at this point that he started to collect books and show a keen interest in rare editions and manuscripts which he

Garden Quadrangle, New College

Wrought Iron Gates, New College

Family Background and Early Years

had specially bound. While he was abroad between 1692 and 1694 he made contacts with agents whom he subsequently employed to collect books and manuscripts for him; and as soon as he acquired quarters of his own in London, he had presses made for his books, and bookplates designed for them. Also, shortly after leaving Oxford, he became a Fellow of the Royal Society, for which some personal merit must have qualified him, since neither his own background nor his relationship to the Willoughby family (Francis Willoughby had been a founder member of the Society) would alone have secured his membership. Subsequently for a number of years he put in assiduous attendance at meetings, and enjoyed the company of fellow members.

In 1692, Brydges was eighteen years old and deemed ready to make a foreign tour, the object of which was to round off his education by enabling him to see something of the world outside England, to meet people of his own class and similar interests, and maybe also to make contacts that socially and politically would prove useful to him in his career. The Grand Tour was not yet the obligatory part of a young man's training that it was to become during the next century, though already it was indulged in often enough for there to be accepted routes to follow, places to visit and experiences to be sought. For those in pursuit of culture, France and Italy were the countries most frequently visited, since in the first could be seen the latest developments in architecture, painting, sculpture and garden planning, and in the second, the original Classical examples which were the inspiration of contemporary trends and enthusiasms. James Brydges however, set off in a different direction, visiting the Low Countries and thence travelling into Germany to Brunswick and Hanover where he spent some time at the Wolfenbottle Academy. He may have returned via France because he certainly had contacts there later on when he wanted to commission the purchase of pictures, materials, snuff-boxes, etc.

Like others travelling abroad at the time, Brydges would have carried letters of introduction to influential people in the places he visited and thus be given the entrée to polite society; and in spite of the fact that the War of the Grand Alliance between France and the United Provinces was in progress, his journey does not seem to have been interrupted in any way. While in Rotterdam he got to know Reineer Leers who was to become one of his chief agents in procuring books and manuscripts; he also began to take an interest in Dutch and Flemish art and to acquire a taste for these. His own preference always seems to have been for religious and narrative paintings, and only after his marriage to Cassandra Willoughby do we find flower and still-life studies among his pictures. In Germany he concentrated on making the acquaintance of people prominent in political life, and especially while in Hanover he cultivated friendships at the court of the Electress Sophia which were to prove useful later, when some of these people accompanied Sophia's son to England to assume sovereignty here in 1714.

Nothing untoward seems to have interrupted Brydges's travels, and he returned – as planned – in 1694 to take up the life of a young man about town; but presently rumours began to reach England of his involvement in a clandestine love affair while abroad, and when his father heard of these he hastily recalled James to Hereford and curtailed his activities for a while. There is no direct evidence of what really happened. Quite often, in spite – or perhaps with the connivance – of their chaperones, young men travelling abroad became involved in romantic escapades which they regarded almost as part of their experience and forgot as quickly as they passed from one place to another. But for a short while the drama of the situation was heightened by resorting to secret meetings and a surreptitious exchange of letters, so that the lovers induced in themselves a feeling of struggling against fate, and incidentally had a ready-made excuse for dropping the whole affair when it became expedient to do so. Four letters, written in French, to Mademoiselle B. and Mademoiselle T. make it seem likely that Brydges did enter into some liaisons during his travels, but not so certain that any ended in marriage, for he would not have regarded lightly such a solemn undertaking, nor callously turned his back on a personal obligation of this kind. The only pointer to the possibility of such a commitment was a further brief visit to Hanover late in 1694, and a letter written on his return to England to Mlle. Alfeldt in which he referred to her as 'a loved wife', and to himself as 'a humble and obedient husband.' This seems to be carrying romanticism – if such it was – to great lengths, yet no more is heard of the lady, and except for Brydges's enforced sojourn at Hereford under the eye of his father, no action was taken by the family in connecton with the affaire.

After this Brydges returned to London where he settled into the pattern of life that he was to follow for a number of years until he had achieved a public position that satisfied him. His father now had a house in Red Lion Square and James stayed here as well as with the Jacob family into which his sister Elizabeth had married. Meanwhile all his activities were geared to furthering his career. He frequented the chocolate houses in St. James's Street and Pall Mall, haunts of the aristocracy, and joined the clubs patronised by those of his own political

Mary Lake and her son John

persuasion, including the Herefordshire Club which met at the Blue Posts in Chancery Lane. Although he was to become an inordinate gambler where business propositions were concerned, he was not addicted to playing cards for high stakes, so there were no attractions for him at White's, Boodles' or Almack's 'where a thousand meadows and cornfields are staked at every throw and as many villages lost as in the earthquakes that overwhelmed Herculaneum and Pompeii'.[7]

Moving in such circles brought home to Brydges the importance of dressing correctly, entertaining with discrimination and being seen in the right places and company at the right time. It was at this point that he began to deal with London tailors, hatters, boot-shoe- and glove-makers, and to attend music meetings, the theatre, private card parties and assemblies. The seriousness of his commitment to this way of life is reflected in the 'Journal' which he kept assiduously from 1696 to 1702 and which consists of little more than lists of places visited, people seen and talked to, and resolutions about future activities. The number of occasions packed into one day and the speed with which he darted from one engagement to another makes *Jennifer's Diary* seem positively dull and uneventful.

> I went and look't in at ye Playhouse: I staid not an act but went hence to Tom's Coffee House.
> After dinner, I went to Lord Pembroke's, who being abroad I went to Lord Arundell, who not being at home I went to Lord Allinton's, but he not being within I went to Mr. Pitt's who being abroad I went to ye Dean of Peterborough's, but he being at church, I went to ye Playhouse in Lincoln's Inn Fields where I met Dr. Davenant and Lord Rumney.[8]

As all this was being written for his private use only, Brydges cannot be accused of name-dropping, but at the end of a day when most of his intended victims were at home, he must surely have indulged in a measure of self-congratulation.

Although it was some while before Brydges was to succeed in his public ambitions, this period of residence in London did see one of his private hopes achieved when he married in 1696, and soon afterwards acquired a home of his own and started a family. His wife was Mary Lake, daughter of Sir Thomas Lake of Stanmore, and like many other arranged marriages, this proved a happy one in spite of the difference in their ages, for she was 30 and he 22. Mary was an affectionate woman, not particularly ambitious nor fond of an active social life but fully

Red Lion Square

Golden Square

Family Background and Early Years

prepared to support her husband in the furtherance of his career. Immediately after their marriage they went to live in Red Lion Square where they began to furnish a house with their own belongings, following the current trend in purchasing upholstered chairs, embroidered quilts, wall-hangings and damask linen while Brydges's own preferences were represented in book-cases, and harpsichord and pictures. 'After dinner we hung up the pictures in the rooms above' was recorded in the 'Journal'. Soon they were to move – as fashion and Brydges's interests dictated – to a larger house in Golden Square, at which point they also acquired a permanent seat in St. James's Church, Piccadilly.

Meanwhile, because of Mary's affection for her family and her husband's growing fondness for the area, they spent their weekends and any free time at Stanmore, where she enjoyed the company of friends and relatives, while he indulged his fondness for bowls, card-playing and socialising with prominent local people, and they both attended the parish church of St. Lawrence at Whitchurch which Brydges was later to rebuild. Only one element of sadness shadowed their lives at this stage, the death – at birth or soon afterwards – of most of the children whom Mary dutifully produced each year.

CHAPTER 2

Political Commitments: 1698–1719

The next stage of James Brydges's life was largely concerned with politics, since most of his time was spent in pursuit of preferment and fulfilling duties connected with the various posts he held. Even his leisure activities were in part directed to the furtherance of his career.

This period covered the last years of William III, the reign of Anne, the accession of George I and the establishment of the Hanoverian dynasty. During the crisis of the Revolution of 1688–9, while prepared to consider some kind of limitation on James II's absolute power, Lord Chandos was not willing to subscribe to the latter's deposition and so he left London for Hereford and thereafter confined his public commitments to local administration.[1] His son did not have the same scruples about transferring his loyalty from one sovereign to another; maybe his staunch Protestantism carried more weight than royalist sympathies in determining his commitment to William III. There is no doubt also that he was already looking ahead to the accession of Anne after the death of her brother-in-law, and making himself as much persona grata with the Princess, her husband George and their entourage, as he tried to be at William's court.

Brydges's first step into active politics was his election to Parliament as a member for Hereford in 1698, a natural consequence of his family's stake in landowning and public service locally, and of its very considerable influence among the electorate both in the county and the city. Even as early as this, well before the corruption of the 18th century House of Commons had reached its height, elections in Herefordshire were notorious. Large sums of money changed hands to secure the votes of the 40sh freeholders in the county and the enfranchised burgesses in the city. 'My agents at Weobley have spoilt the business by giving money barefacedly' reported one candidate. In addition, threats were used to ensure the support of potentially independent electors, and mutually slanderous attacks made by the candidates.

Unexpectedly, despite the advantage of family influence, James Brydges was not returned unopposed in 1698, and his reaction to the situation was characteristically revealing. Initially he was taken aback that Sir Thomas Southwell was standing against him, and then he was affronted when his opponent began to throw an unflattering light on some of his (Brydges's) activities in town, hinting at his unsuitability as a prospective member – 'a great courtier, who would certainly be a pensioner if once chosen Parliament man'. Refusing to admit to himself or anyone else that his methods of seeking advancement might well be interpreted in this way, Brydges tried to arrange a meeting with Sir Thomas in order to persuade him to retract his accusations. Eventually, but not without considerable trouble that must have caused much amusement among the onlookers, Brydges caught up not with Sir Thomas himself but with his brother, and the matter was brought to an amicable conclusion. Brydges was always excessively sensitive to criticism, whether this was justified or not; and three years later, when there was another election and more mud was slung – not at himself this time but at his father – he went as far as challenging his opponent to a duel, an even more ludicrous affair than his pursuit of Sir Thomas Southwell, that ended with Brydges disarming his opponent, then offering him both weapons back, and finally going off with him arm-in-arm to dinner.

However, the achievement of a Parliamentary seat, although it bestowed prestige and a certain importance both locally and in London, was merely the opening gambit in what Brydges hoped would prove a successful (and lucrative) power game. 'Office cannot fail of bringing one a vast fortune'. Prior to his election, he had already got himself presented to William III and introduced to Prince George of Denmark, hoping that being thus known in court circles might secure him a post in the Excise department. It was perhaps his failure in this project that helped to persuade him that membership of Parliament might be a better starting point for preferment. At any rate, during the next five years he put in regular attendance when Parliament was in session and soon earned a reputation as a diligent committee man, willing to take an interest and serve in whatever matters were demanding attention, though it was noticeable that increasingly he took an interest in maritime affairs, seeking the company and cultivating the acquaintance of men connected with naval administration, efforts which were rewarded in 1703 by his being made one of the Commissioners of the Admiralty under the direction of Prince George.

Except for a conscientious application to business in hand, we know

Prince George of Denmark

nothing outstanding of Brydges's contribution to Admiralty affairs: and possibly there is not more to be known, since already his mind was turning to further promotion in a different sphere. Two years earlier the country had embarked on the War of the Spanish Succession, partly because of Louis XIV's flagrant breach of promises made in the Partition Treaties that the Spanish Empire should not pass undivided to a French prince, but much more because English business men and merchants could see a promise of economic gain in a successful war against France and Spain. They envisaged a struggle wherein the English navy would establish its supremacy in the Channel and seas around Britain as well as in American and West Indian waters, and thus make all these parts safe for English shipping and trade. But though there was some naval activity, and coastal raids on the French and Spanish coasts successfully kept large numbers of French troops occupied at a distance from the main scenes of action, the war was primarily a military one, fought on several fronts, its course very much determined by the strategy of the Duke of Marlborough who led the allied British and Dutch forces. At home therefore, the main interest necessarily centred on the conduct of the land war and those connected with it; and Brydges who was already acquainted with the Duke of Marlborough began to entertain the idea of improving his prospects through the latter. His commitments in Parliament and acquaintances at court enabled him to learn of coming vacancies in government offices, and by 1705 he had left the Admiralty to take up the position of Paymaster to the Queen's Forces abroad, a promotion for which he acknowledged his indebtedness to Marlborough, 'whose noble friendship and mediation has placed me where I am.'

Satisfaction over his appointment led Brydges to make one of his characteristic, impulsive gestures. In addition to expressing his gratitude in letters to Marlborough himself, he sent a gift to the Duchess, a ring of such obvious worth that it caused acute embarrassment and prompted her refusal to accept 'what I would not take from any person I know but the Queen and the Duke.' So uncomfortable did she feel that she wrote to the Duke to sound his views on what had happened. He replied:

> I find the present of Mr. Brydges of a much greater value than I could have wished. I really do not know what to advise you, but I think your letter is very well till you can see him, and I shall take care to send it to him.[2]

The accession of Queen Anne in 1702 had brought back into power and prominence the Tory politicians and High Churchmen who had been out of favour under William III, and during the early years of the reign it was mainly these men who filled ministerial posts and advised the Queen on governmental affairs – always with the object of recovering some of the ground they had lost to their Whig rivals during the previous reign. But although the Queen herself was in agreement with the outlook and sentiments of the Tories and would – from choice – have acquiesced readily in whatever policies they advocated, circumstances prevented complete co-operation between them. Representing the landed classes, their dependants and members of the Church of England, the Tories regarded the war to which the country was committed as unprofitable and a totally unnecessary expense, since they did not share their rivals' dislike and distrust of Louis XIV's absolutism, Catholicism and friendship for the exiled Stuarts, and had no particular interest in overseas trade. Had it not been for the Duchess of Marlborough's influence over the Queen (she was considerably more of a Whig than her husband) and the government's dependence for money on the Bank of England and London business men, Tory influence – represented by Robert Harley and Henry St. John – might have prevailed completely, but as it was, some Whigs remained in office (notably Godolphin at the Treasury) and continued to support the war and the Duke of Marlborough who was conducting it. As long as the ministry reflected both points of view, so members of Parliament were divided in their loyalties (ministries were formed before elections and largely determined the outcome of these) but gradually war fever, fanned by Marlborough's series of victories at Blenheim, Ramillies, Oudenarde and Malplaquet, swept the country, and by 1708 neither in the ministry nor in Parliament nor among the people at large was anti-war sentiment being expressed. Marlborough, although a Tory at heart, had to ally himself with those who were ready to support and further his campaigns: his wife kept the Queen's interests focussed on the war: Harley and St. John, luke-warm enthusiasts, were dropped from the ministry and replaced by whole-hearted Whigs.

Although never prominent in ministerial activities nor in a position to influence policies, Brydges was nevertheless quite close to the centre of events. His aunt, Beata Danvers, was a lady-in-waiting to the Queen and influential at court; and the Brydges were on terms of friendship with the Godolphins who in turn were related to the Marlboroughs, so a kind of family network was operating in his favour. Brydges certainly appreciated having a working relationship with Godolphin and continued to feel indebted to Marlborough. After the election of 1708, when his seat at

Henry St John, Viscount Bolingbroke

Sir Robert Walpole

Hereford had been challenged by one 'sufficiently versed in the art of undermining', he expressed his gratitude to them both in a letter to Marlborough:

> I beg leave to own, with the deepest sense of respect and gratitude, that I reckoned it one of the most pleasing and happy accidents of my whole life, when I found myself so much the care of the two greatest men this kingdom has produced.

It should perhaps be mentioned that on this occasion Brydges's opponents had much the same things to say of his methods as he of theirs, and in spite of his expressed disapproval of borough-mongering, it was a case of the pot calling the kettle black. Whether he was seeking support on his own account, or as later on behalf of his son, Brydges evidently resorted to all the known devices for winning votes. Thomas Foley, one of the contestants at Hereford in 1708 wrote this to Robert Harley:

> I will not be wanting in endeavour to keep up my interest at Hereford though it will be a near struggle. Mr. Brydges's agents aim much more to put me out than Mr. Morgan . . . their practices being the most obnoxious I ever knew in any case whatever. His extravagant expenses may gain him numbers which at present I know he wants.[3]

Meanwhile, secure in his appointment at the Paymaster's Office and with the help of a number of influential friends, Brydges was making the most of his opportunities. At that time, for anyone who had put himself out to achieve high place, it would have seemed extraordinary not to seek some return for effort expended, a means of livelihood for the present and a measure of insurance against an uncertain future. Brydges was no exception to this rule save that his efforts to exploit the possibilities of the Paymaster's Office met with a success that seemed outstanding even for those days. As Onslow recorded:

> He was the most surprising instance of a change of fortune raised by a man himself, that has happened I believe in any age. When he came first into the office of Paymaster of the army, he had little or no estate of his own and never inherited more than a few hundred pounds a year, but by means of this office and the improvements of money, in little more than ten years, living expensively too in the meanwhile, he had accumulated a fortune of not less than six or seven hundred thousand pounds.

The opportunities available to Brydges and his close colleagues were twofold; they were handling money that did not have to be accounted for in the immediate future, and they had access to inside information that could be used as a basis for speculation. Firstly, money for war expenditure was drafted to the Paymaster's Office at the start of each financial year to be spent as and when needs dictated; so by 'borrowing' some of this for investment until it had to be spent officially, Brydges was able to collect interest on capital sums to which he would never have had access as a private individual. Often too, the payment of bills to foreign creditors could be delayed until the rates of exchange were in favour of the British debtor; or else advantage taken of the varying rates of exchange to buy up foreign currency at cheap rates and hold it until it could be paid out at a higher one. Secondly, precise and reliable information about the movements of the army, future campaigns, or the prospects of peace were obtained by Brydges through Lord Cadogan, Marlborough's aide and confidant: and at a time when a mania for speculation had already begun to sweep the country and the most far-fetched and illusory schemes could beguile investors, it was not difficult to launch lotteries connected with more realistic possibilities, e.g. whether the army would next proceed to another battle or a siege: and whether peace would be signed in six months, a year, or longer. Within the accepted bounds, Brydges certainly went as far as he could to do well for himself out of his appointment, yet when we consider the vast sums of money that passed through his hands and for which he was ultimately answerable, his gains from the office seem quite modest; and it must be acknowledged that although after his resignation attempts were made to bring charges of misappropriation against him, none of these could be or were ever proved, and in view of Brydges's habitual timidity when he was exercising his own judgment or initiative, it seems most unlikely that he would ever have made a really successful criminal on a large scale.

That enthusiasm for the war had depended to quite a large extent on Whig propaganda and Marlborough's spectacular victories became apparent when activities abroad began to settle into a dull routine of sieges and when the expenses of military and naval commitments had to be met by increased taxation. Boredom and apathy set in as quickly as enthusiasm had mounted previously. As Henry St. John commented in a letter to Brydges: 'God only knows what is expected in this restless unsatisfied Country of ours, but I heare it already everywere said that if the Campaign is spent in Sieges, it will only serve to lay the foundation of another.' All the same another factor helped to bring about the downfall of the Whig ministry that had supported the war; this was the supersession of the Duchess of Marlborough in the Queen's affections by Abigail Masham, a distant relative of Robert Harley and a lady-in-waiting, whose influence on behalf of the Tories led to ministerial changes which then brought a Tory majority into Parliament too. As chief protagonist of the war Marlborough was the main target of attack, but those who had been associated with him were also in line for censure, as this letter from Brydges to Godolphin in May 1710 forecast:

> I cannot be so slight an observer of what passes in the world as not to perceive there is a party forming to disturb the measures of those who have done so much at home and abroad to promote the welfare of the publick and perhaps to take no notice of it to your Lordship may argue me of indifference in a cause, which if I did not enter into with the utmost zeal and warmth, I might be justly thought the most ungrateful man alive.
> I am wholly ignorant of what resolutions other gentlemen may have taken, who are in the same bottom with me, but I hope both your Lordship and the Duke of Marlborough will do me the justice to rest assured that as I owe the progress I have made in business and the improvements of my estate to your joint goodness, so in the case of those changes at Court which are talked of, when your service calls for it I shall lay down my employment with as much cheerfulness as I came first into it, believing it the greatest happiness and honour that can befall me to run their fortune who have so nobly contributed to the establishment of mine.[4]

Shortly after this, Lord Sunderland, Secretary of State (and Marlborough's son-in-law) and Lord Treasurer Godolphin were dismissed and it was generally anticipated that others, including Brydges, would resign before being overtaken by a similar fate. However, despite expectations and his own declared intention, the latter not only clung to office but also braved the mounting criticism of his own conduct and popular discrediting of Marlborough. This stand was not maintained without much soul-searching however. Letters passed between Brydges and Godolphin with the former protesting: 'I cannot without concern observe I am so much the object of some people's anger'. Yet he was soon in correspondence with Robert Harley, (distantly related to the Brydges family, though the kinship had never been much publicised or exploited before), justifying his clinging to office by maintaining: 'I am much abler to defend myself if I am in than I should be if I were out of my post. To do me any prejudice, malice must be very unjust and potent.' Harley, back in office, but not yet confident of a following, was prepared to justify him by making his case a special one: 'I can only say I would have thought of separating your case from that of others, which is the true way to do you justice.' Thus did he help to save Brydges – and gain himself a supporter. Meanwhile Brydges's decision to stay in office was also endorsed by friends and members of his family who believed that resignation would look like an admission of guilt, and the sharing of disgrace with Godolphin and Marlborough merely vain knight-errantry. His brother-in-law, Theophilus Leigh, commenting on the situation in letters to his son, implied that there were others much more deserving of blame than Brydges and added: 'I doubt not but it is a busy time with your uncle Brydges. I long to hear that he comes off well with his Accounts in Parliament.'

Harley, who had been made Earl of Oxford on taking over Godolphin's post as Lord Treasurer, now held the chief power in the ministry along with Henry St. John, Viscount Bolingbroke, and together they started moves to end the war and reach a peaceful settlement of the issues involved. Necessarily Marlborough was dismissed since to him such negotiations were akin to treason, and this might well have heightened the precariousness of Brydges's position. But the latter was already working in reasonable harmony with Oxford and Bolingbroke, and meanwhile had secured the good offices of the new favourite, Mrs. Masham, probably more through the influence of his aunt Beata Danvers than thanks to his own efforts which included the gift to Mrs. Masham of 'a trifle of dressing plate' – in fact, an embarrassingly expensive offering. Certainly by the time Marlborough's downfall was complete in 1712, Brydges was on sufficiently friendly terms with Mrs. Masham to write to her of his innermost feelings and convictions:

> The Duke of Marlborough's business in Parliament has put me under very great difficulties. The obligations I have to his Grace are known to all the world. His favour first raised me to what I am and I cannot leave him in his present troubles without incurring the censure of ingratitude. On the other hand, to appear in the defence of one who is so unfortunate as to lie under the Queen's displeasure, while I am actually in her service, carries with it such an air of indecency as every gentleman ought to avoid. . . .
> I shall not forsake my principles. I shall inviolably preserve my duty to the Queen in the House of Commons and in the House of Peers

The Duke of Marlborough

The Duchess of Marlborough

when succession brings me thither. I shall constantly adhere to the notions of government wherein I and all my family have been educated, which are immovable fidelity to my sovereign and zeal for the Church of England, not to be shaken by the arts or power of faction.[5]

Maybe there is an element of special pleading here, but compared with some of Brydges's more affected and obsequious letters, this has an unusual ring of truth and sincerity.

It was not until 1713 that Brydges resigned his position as Paymaster, by which time he had proved that he was not afraid to face any consequences of his activities in office. There were other motives too, behind the decision that he made at this point. The conclusion of peace negotiations at Utrecht in 1713 meant that the forces abroad would soon be brought home and the role of a Paymaster no longer necessary. Moreover, the Queen's precarious state of health was making the future of paramount importance to the politicians, and with a total disregaard for the sovereign's feelings, members of the two parties openly discussed their respective hopes – the Tories, of retaining the Stuart dynasty by negotiating with James Edward, Anne's half-brother, to return to England: the Whigs, of ensuring that the terms of the Revolution Settlement should be fulfilled and Sophia of Hanover or her son George enabled to succeed to the throne. Of these two plans Brydges was inclined to favour the second, because of his commitment to the Church of England and perhaps also because he had already made friends at the Hanoverian court while he was in Germany and was by no means perturbed at the idea of some of these people constituting the English court. So as Oxford and Bolingbroke were making an approach to James Edward, Brydges necessarily had to detach himself from them.

When in 1714 Anne finally died it was the Whigs who acted the more promptly and expeditiously, so that George of Hanover was all ready to set off for England before James Edward had even finished discussing the prospect of such a move with his followers. Meanwhile, the centre of attention and activity in London was the household of Baron von Bothmer, the Hanoverian ambassador to England since 1710, with whom the leading Whigs and Brydges were all on friendly terms, and through whom they had been maintaining contact with Hanover. Thus when the Elector first arrived, a coterie of potential friends and supporters was all ready to welcome him. George, who was retiring by nature and hated to be the centre of attention, probably did not regret that the

Robert Harley, Earl of Oxford

last part of his journey – up the Thames to Greenwich – was completed in a thick fog, nor that it was dark when he finally reached London, so that although 'a vast mob and crowd lined the streets and there were great bonfires and illuminations at night, they had not the satisfaction of seeing his Majesty.' While he was still at Greenwich many courtiers and Whig politicians went down river to greet him, Brydges among them; and two days later, when the new King made his first triumphal procession through London, Brydges was 'one in the Cavalcade which attended him through the City.' Clearly Brydges was already in favour with England's new sovereign, for within a month he had procured for his father the additional titles of Viscount Wilton and Earl of Caernarvon, which fate decreed should immediately be transferred to himself, since Lord Chandos died the day after these honours had been bestowed.

George I's establishment in England, only momentarily threatened by the Jacobite rebellion of 1715, secured the return to office of those who had been discredited and dismisseed during the last years of Anne's reign. Godolphin had died in 1712, but Sunderland, Townsend and Walpole were included in the King's Council and Marlborough was reinstated as Captain General of the Army, the King having expressed the wish: 'My dear Duke, I hope you have now seen the end of your troubles.' Closer to George than any of these though, were Baron von Bothmer, the advisers he had brought with him from Hanover – Baron von Bernstorff and Jean de Robothen, and his two mistresses – Melusina von Schulenberg afterwards Duchess of Kendal, and Sophia Kielmansegge, afterwards Countess of Darlington. Those who sought favours or promotion or merely the ear of the King, usually did so through one of these. Benefits and offices were not openly bought or sold, but there is no doubt that considerable sums of money and payments in kind passed through the hands of those close to the King. Brydges always maintained that he wanted to get on through his own merit and the King's goodness 'without such an intervention of his Ministers as will lay me under the obligation of an entire dependence upon them and an absolute resignation of myself to their measures.' Nevertheless, Mesdames von Schulenberg and Kielmansegge received from him gifts of jewellery, wine and sweetmeats, together with sums of money, as did Bernstorff; and Bothmer's sweetener was Brydges's agreement to buy two horses from him at a price fixed by Bothmer himself. There was no overt link between this liberality and the sinecures Brydges subsequently acquired, but some of the offers he was made could only have come through the favour of one of those near the King, who were in a position to dispense such patronage.

Being out of office and having relinquished his seat in the Commons on inheriting his father's titles, Brydges was now looking elsewhere for an interest and a lucrative source of income. A position at Court meant honour, profit and opportunities for frequent contact with the King, but he did not really want any appointment that would absorb too much of his time. A Treasurership of the Chamber he would have considered 'because it would trouble him so little', but this did not come his way. When offered the Comptrollership, he declined to accept because of

> 'the attendance and also the expense it requires. Everyone who has had it yet, as I remember, have not only attended constantly at Court in town but likewise at Windsor and wherever the Court happens to be which will by no means agree with my temper: besides the hurry one must always be in upon great days at Court.'[6]

The appointments that he did take up in the end – as Clerk of the Hanaper and of the Sixpenny Writs – brought him regular if not vast salaries, and they were certainly undemanding of his time and energies.

Brydges's reference to the time-consuming aspect and expense of being in constant attendance on the King, reflects the demands made on aspiring courtiers. Although George, as far as possible, avoided leading his life publicly and kept to his small circle of Hanoverian friends, nevertheless his Court was a conventional one where great importance was attached to the formal celebration of such occasions as his birthday, the anniversary of his coronation and so on. Macky, a contemporary commentator, reported:

> The King's birthday (is) observed with the utmost splendour at Court. The Nobility and Gentry of both sexes make their Equipages on this solemn Occasion, striving to outvie one another in magnificence, new Coaches and Liveries; and the Noblemen, Gentlemen and Ladies wait upon his Majesty in the greatest sumptuousness that can be expressed.[7]

Proper dress being the sine qua non of admission to the Court at all times, the expense of this necessarily excluded some people from attendance altogether, or else made their occasional appearances something in the nature of an investment. Writing to Lady Cowper, who – because of her husband's illness – had been unable to attend a birthday celebration for the Princess of Wales, the Duchess of Marlborough counselled:

The Palace of St James's

James Brydges, Duke of Chandos

Since you have made the clothes and everybody in the World knows your present circumstances, it will be just as well to put them on the first day you can easily wait upon the Princess and show her how fine you were to have been.

The rigidity of court etiquette also explains the anxiety of Brydges's second wife Cassandra to avoid being thought remiss in failing to attend upon the Princess of Wales, as revealed in a letter to the Countess of Suffolk:

I must entreat your pardon for the favour I am going to ask of your Ladyship which is that when you next go to the Princess, you will give me leave to wait upon you, for since her Royal Highness came to England, I have not been well enough to venture to Court and shall now need an advocate to get me presented to her.

She also wished to observe the convention in respect of court mourning. Her housekeeper Mrs. Oakley, evidently entrusted to make the necessary enquiries, reported:

Your Grace's Black Padua Soye Mantoe and Petticoat will be sent to Canons with my Lady Caernarvon's fringed headdress. I could not ask ye Vice Chamberlain about ye Lady's mourning, but his Porter who is well-styled in these sorts of affairs told me ye Ladies are to wear ye same headdress as before ye Coronation Day viz Edged linen.

The absence of a Queen (George had divorced his wife and left her imprisoned in Germany) and the strained relationship between the King and his heir the Prince of Wales, also added to the difficulties of court life and called for extreme tact and diplomacy on the part of those hoping to ensure both their present position and future prospects. The King's preference for seclusion precluded many activities – receptions and entertainments for instance – usually associated with the Court, and encouraged those who expected such social pleasures, to seek them in the company of the Prince of Wales to whom 'the pageantry and splendour, the badges and trappings of royalty, were as pleasing as they were irksome to his father' (Harvey). His apartments at St. James's were always open, and his wife held evening drawing-rooms, arranged musical entertainments and gave balls. George, always suspicious of any potentially political moves made by his son, was prepared to allow him this social success, except for a time between 1717 and 1719 when he returned from a visit to Hanover to find the Prince consorting closely with some disaffected politicians. Realising the importance of recovering lost ground and of superseding his son, George embarked on a period of intensive social activity and hospitality, 'maintaining a magnificent public table at vast expense at St. James's, in Parliament time, for the entertainment of members, organising concerts and balls, hiring a company from Drury Lane to perform plays, and himself very obliging and in great humour'. But even when remote from the scene in his habitual seclusion, the King was well aware of all that was going on and it behoved those who wished to remain in royal favour to be sparing in the attention that they gave to the Prince. While keeping in with the latter through his wife's attendance on the Princess, Brydges himself remained more closely in touch with the King through his Hanoverian entourage, and was rewarded for his assiduity in 1719 when he achieved what was to prove the height of his success, and was raised to the peerage with the title Duke of Chandos.

CHAPTER 3

Business Associates And Family Life

During the years of commitment to political affairs, Brydges did not altogether abandon other interests and pursuits. Especially after 1714, when suitable sinecures were slow to materialise, he was drawn increasingly into the world of business with the idea of improving his fortunes by exploiting the contacts he had there and any opportunities that might come his way.

In the early part of the 18th century, to an unprecedented degree, the country was becoming aware of the importance of trade and of the fortunes to be made from it – hence the enthusiasm among the mercantile classes for the War of the Spanish Succession: the growing significance of the City of London, where the bulk of the nation's commercial business was conducted: and the gradual domination of politics by those who had ready money to lend to the government or invest in official schemes. 'Our merchants are princes, greater, richer and more powerful than some sovereign princes.' News of trading companies, of possible speculations and of new ventures overseas dominated the conversation in City coffee-houses and round the dining tables of City magnates and of the gentry and aristocracy with whom they consorted; and the fervour that a century earlier had gone into defending religious or political beliefs was now directed into formulating and upholding economic theories in respect of trade and its connection with national well-being.

As we have noticed, there were several successful business men among Brydges's relatives. Sir Henry Barnard, his grandfather, was a leading member of the Turkey Company, one of those whose influence had helped to secure Lord Chandos's appointment as ambassador to Constantinople where the latter was in a position to further the interests of the Company as well as those of his country. (Was it Barnard who persuaded him to 'let his whiskers grow after the manner agreeable to the Turks and used by the nation there'?). Alexander Jacob, the husband of Brydges's sister Elizabeth, was also a member of the Turkey Company.

Thus even after his grandfather's death in 1680, Brydges retained his links with and interest in the affairs of the company. During the late 17th and early 18th centuries, England's trade in the Mediterranean and with the Far East via Mediterranean ports was not as important as it had been earlier, nevertheless the Turkey Company remained useful in that it could satisfy the demand for luxuries such as carpets and silks, and necessities such as spices and dyes. Moreover, its overheads were not nearly as expensive as those of companies trading outside Europe, so that its invested capital was both secure and profit-making, and worthy of Brydges's notice.

Another relative much admired by Brydges was Sir Josiah Child, a man who from humble beginnings had made a spectacularly successful career in business, and progressed through a directorship to be Governor of the East India Company. He had clear-cut economic beliefs as well as great ability, and according to Macaulay 'into whatever errors he may occasionally have fallen as a theorist, it is certain that, as a practical man of business, he had few equals.' Under his direction the Company went from strength to strength, and the fortunes made by its shareholders (mostly friends and relations of the Governor himself) roused such jealousy and enmity as to cause a public outcry for an end to its monopoly. Tough, astute and ruthless, Sir Josiah was held in awe rather than liked by those with whom he had dealings. Cassandra Willoughby, his step-daughter and Brydges's second wife, was no doubt echoing popular admiration for his business acumen when, after a visit to Portsmouth in 1697, she reported in her 'Journal':

> The Market Place, I thought ye Hansomest building I saw in ye town, and it was built by Sir Josiah Child when he was Mayor there, without putting ye Town to any charge, for he agreed with ye undertaker of ye work to be at ye whole expense and that for it he should have a lease of all ye stalls for such a terme of years and after that time was expired, ye Town should have ye advantage of it, which they now have and get a good income by, without ever being at any expense for ye building.

Certainly, her own opinion and that of her brothers was less favourable, since their step-father unscrupulously engrossed all the revenues of the Willoughby estates when he married their mother, and only after prolonged legal action returned the family properties to the rightful heir.

However, by whatever means he achieved it, there is no doubt that Child's wealth made him a formidable figure in the business world and

Sir Josiah Child

Sir Hans Sloane

enabled him also to set himself up among the gentry who were acquiring country houses outside London (in his case at Wanstead, Essex) and renovating these and their grounds according to current fashions. In addition riches brought social prestige in their train. Thus it was possible for Child's daughter Rebecca to marry the Marquis of Worcester, and his grand-daughter, Elizabeth Howland, the Duke of Bedford's heir. Through Sir Josiah, Brydges acquired an interest in the East India Company, which survived the vicissitudes of its fortunes during the early years of Anne's reign, and in due course not only brought him a return on his investments, but also gave him access to the silks, jewels (Brydges liked diamonds), calicoes and spices that were the company's stock-in-trade.

Brydges also had investments in the Royal African Company. Like the East India Company, this was a joint-stock venture, requiring large amounts of financial capital to meet the expenses of forts, warehouses, armed merchant vessels and long voyages, more money in fact than could be raised by a limited number of merchants. In the late 17th century, the Company had attracted the particular interest of the Court, and a large amount of its stock was held by aristocracy and gentry. Cargoes of cloth and metal wares were exchanged on the Guinea coast for slaves, gold dust and ivory which were then sold against sugar, rum and tobacco in the West Indies and southern colonies in America. Brydges was not only interested in the company's established lines of business, but anxious also to increase the scope of these if possible. To this end he enlisted the aid of Sir Hans Sloane, a friend of the Willoughby family, a member of the Royal Society and medical consultant to the royal family, who therefore moved in the same circles as Brydges. Trained as a physician, Sloane had also made an extensive study of tropical plants and was an inveterate collector of curiosities, so when Brydges wanted information about hitherto unknown and untried products, it was to Sloane that he turned. Would the latter please interview a man said 'to understand the nature of plants and drugs pretty well' and decide 'whether he is proper for the business he is recommended for' – that is, to go to Africa to discover 'some useful plants or drugs or weeds that might be better known'.

Sloane was also asked to 'cast his eye over some specimens of drugs and plants we are going to send to our settlements abroad in order to make enquiry among the Natives and Negroes brought down to be sold, whether their country produces any such.' Would Sloane please decide 'whether there are any in this Catalogue too common to be worth the enquiry or if there are any others proper to be included.' Evidently

Brydges obtained some promising specimens, because in another letter to Sloane he offered to show him 'samples of herbs and roots said to be of sovereign virtues . . . . . also a balsame (of which one of the ingredients is Palm oil) which they use with great success for ye cure of ye Gout and Gangrene.' In addition he asked for some instructions 'to find out for their better preserving and ordering, the plants they send which by the length of the Voyages become mouldy and rotten; as also proper directions for finding and eating ye Snakes root plant and Dragonsblood which I take to be the gum of ye Palm trees, as also a receipt to extract Turpentine out of any trees yielding it, and what is ye proper season for so doing.'[1]

In addition to Brydges's acquaintance with plants, his correspondence with Sloane throws interesting light on the activities of the African Company. It took three months to get the slaves from the interior to the coast where they were sold; six to twelve months was allowed for a round voyage from London to Africa and thence to the West Indies and home again. The company entered into contracts with suitable qualified botanists to investigate all the potentialities of their holdings, 'so that the voyage in all probability will prove the making of fortunes.' And was there an 18th century equivalent of closed shop agreements in operation, since the African Company had to obtain 'a lycense from the East India Company to carry ye two African Princes home to their own Country'?

The three companies mentioned so far were all well-established by the beginning of the 18th century, and short of untoward disasters caused by bad weather at sea or hostile natives, any investment in them was fairly certain to be rewarded. Newer, untried ventures held greater risks, though returns on their stocks could be considerable if all went well. Brydges concerned himself with two of these. The first was the Mississippi Company, started in France by a Scotsman John Law, who secured government support for his scheme and a few years of success before it finally foundered. Among those whom Brydges entrusted with commissions abroad was John Drummond, and through him £40,000 was invested in the company. The Drummonds were an interesting family. Their banking business had been started by Andrew a cousin of John who had come from Scotland and settled in London early in the 18th century.[2] They lived at Stanmore where Zoffany painted them en famille and where they were among the friends whose company Brydges enjoyed when he went out of town. He and John Drummond were in the habit of doing each other good turns and they evidently valued their friendship. A letter to Brydges from Drummond in Amsterdam, dated 1710, ran as follows:

The Drummond Family at Stanmore

> My worthy good friend Monsr Cals's 2 sons going into England, as he is the first Banquier of this place and one who has been extreamly obliging to me in all the course of my business here, I cannot but shew my respects to his sons who are become his partners, by recommending them to some of my best friends in England and I am sure I cannot do it in a better manner than by giving them the opportunity of kissing your hands, if you'd be so kind to accept a recommendation from such a mean person who will always esteem it his happiness to be reckoned among your humble servants. They are two modest, pretty young Gentlemen and they will be extream fond of seeing the Court and the Queen on any publick day in the Drawing Room or going or coming from the Chapell.[3]

The other new venture into which Brydges flung himself was the South Sea Company, formed to exploit the trade advantage secured for England by the Treaty of Utrecht. From the start, the company had great momentum behind it, and those who could afford invested vast sums in it. Interest in the company and competition to acquire stock in it amounted almost to a frenzy, as Edward Harley reported in a letter to his father:

> The town is quite mad about the South Sea, some losers, some great gainers, one can hear nothing else talked of. It is being very unfashionable not to be in the South Sea. I have heard but one sound these three months in this place, viz that of South Sea which has got the better of men's politics and ladies' fashions and has entirely engrossed all conversation.
> No one is satisfied with even exorbitant gain but everyone thirsts for more.[4]

Cassandra Willoughby, Brydges's second wife, brought £11,000 in South Sea stock with her as part of her dowry and her mother had an even larger stake in the company. Brydges too had South Sea stock at the time of his marriage to Cassandra in 1713 and added to it in due course. In this venture he had Sir Robert Walpole to steer him. The latter had been a governmental colleague during Anne's reign and remained a friend whom Brydges entertained regularly and consulted in financial matters. Although Walpole was to be the chief minister of George I and George II during the 1720's and 1730's, by which time Brydges was out of office, nevertheless the latter must have seemed close to Walpole as he was frequently approached with requests to use his influence with the minister.

Unlike Walpole, who skilfully and just in time, extricated himself from involvement in the affairs of the South Sea Company, Brydges was among those with money still invested (in his case £50,000) when the Company collapsed in 1720. That many were completely ruined by the Bubble is unquestionable: and that others were obliged to abandon plans calling for the expenditure of wealth that had not materialised, is also true.

> This town is in a very shattered condition, eleven out of the twelve Judges are dipped in South Sea: Bishops, Deans and Doctors, in short everybody that had money. Some of the Quality are quite broke. Coaches and equipages are laying down every day and 'tis expected that the Christmas Holydays will be very melancholy.

The attempts of Brydges's wife to borrow money from various friends to tide him over a lean period would seem to argue that he too had been hard hit, but a further passage from the letter quoted above, written by William Brydges who was in London in November 1720, throws a different light on the situation:

> By his (Brydges's) behaviour, he does not seem to be affected by the fall of Stocks and I am sure by what I've learnt, he is noe otherwise a loser than by not making up of the advantage he might have taken in disposing when things were in a flourishing condition. Whatever the opinion may be here or with you as to his losses, he has within this fortnight bought or bid for two estates in Hampshire – £800 p.a. value, he has likewise lately bought the manner (manor) of Tufton below Burlip (Birdlip) in Gloucester, and also Downton near Kineton value £400 p.a. This does not seem to favour the late current, though some of his own friends go into that stream, because I beleive that it may be fashionable as well as politic to be a loser with the rest of the world.[5]

Meanwhile as a essential background to his business commitments, Brydges strove to maintain a satisfactory family life. Soon after his marriage to Mary Lake in 1696, he began the habit of moving house from time to time so as to have a convenient base for his activities and an establishment commensurate with his growing importance and prestige. So Red Lion Square was abandoned in 1700 for Golden Square, and this for Albemarle Street in 1712; but following the current fashion, Brydges also took on an out-of-town house, Sion Hill at Isleworth, which he rented from the Duke of Somerset and where he first started to indulge his taste for grandeur. Although the house and its grounds were not his own, Brydges drew up elaborate plans for improving the garden and embellishing the interior of the house. Fruit-trees and flowers were introduced into the former, and seeds obtained from Holland to stock herb and kitchen gardens. Blue and white tiles were bought also in Holland and shipped to England to make fireplaces and line cupboards. Tapestry and linens came from Brussels: damask and velvet for hangings and curtains from Italy. Interesting as an indication of Brydges's personal tastes at the time were his purchases of manuscripts through Renier Leers of Amsterdam and pictures through his nephew William Leigh, and the formation of a library of which the nucleus consisted of Lord Clarendon's collection of books.

Relations between Brydges and the ducal owner of Sion Hill became strained in due course (did Somerset feel that the alterations amounted to a criticism of his own management of the property?) and perhaps it was as well that Brydges had meanwhile found a country home of his own which enabled him to give up Sion Hill. The new acquisition was Canons Park at Edgware, purchased from Sir Lancelot Lake, his wife's uncle. Mary Lake unfortunately died in 1712, shortly before Brydges bought the house, so she never enjoyed life there with her husband. We shall look more carefully at the development of Canons in due course, sufficient here to notice that for a number of years after 1713, the rebuilding and furnishing of the house and the beautifying of its surroundings constituted an engrossing and satisfying interest for Brydges.

The purchase of Canons was completed almost simultaneously with Brydges's second marriage to his cousin Cassandra, daughter of Francis Willoughby and Emma Barnard. The wedding, conducted by Brydges's brother Henry, took place in the chapel belonging to the Chelsea Hospital in October 1713, a quiet ceremony attended only by Cassandra's mother and a few friends. Brydges had known Cassandra for a long time as they had often been fellow guests at the homes of the Barnards, the Childs and Brydges's own parents, and there is no reason to doubt his statement that his respect and liking for her had grown over the years. That Cassandra, who was 43 years old, had never been married before, is strange in view of her ample fortune (about £23,000) but as a young woman, after her mother's second marriage to Sir Josiah Child, she had been fully occupied in running the family home at Wollaton for each of her two brothers in turn: and later, in taking concerned interest in her

Cassandra Willoughby, 1st Duchess of Chandos

mother, the children of her brother Thomas and her half-brother Sir Richard Child. Brydges's decision to marry again within a year of his first wife's death may explain the secrecy that surrounded preparations for the ceremony; he also seems to have been somewhat sensitive about Cassandra's age, since in enlisting the help of his nephew to buy materials in Paris for the bride's trousseau, he was at pains to emphasise that these must be suitable for someone of mature years and taste. However, it is certain that both entered upon the marriage with high hopes, as Brydges reported in a letter to his cousin Francis Brydges:

> I make no question but your wishes for Mrs. Brydges's and my happiness in each other will be very successfull. I hope there is nothing in my nature that can render her life uncomfortable and I am sure there is everything in hers I can desire to make me perfectly fortunate.[6]

And although it must have been a source of disappointment to both that there were no children of the union, husband and wife settled into a very comfortable routine, he admiring and respectful of her integrity, artistic ability and practical good sense: she ready to support him in his ambitions, to tolerate his moods as they varied with his fortunes and to shield him (if she could) from the consequences of his mistakes.

The early years of the marriage were spent between Brydges's town house in Albemarle Street and the new one at Canons, the former being used for entertaining and as a convenient pied-a-terre while the latter was in process of being rebuilt and furnished, and its management arranged. Cassandra had already had considerable experience in housekeeping, and to choose appropriate furnishings and make some of these herself, appoint servants and oversee the domestic economy presented no difficulty to her. Nor does she seem to have been put out by the countless journeys made between Albemarle Street and Canons. While living with her brother she had spent much of her time travelling on horseback with him to inspect the family estates and to visit spas and places of interest, so the distance between London and Edgware, covered in a coach, was no hardship. Brydges was always admiring of Cassandra's good taste and industry in domestic matters, as she was appreciative of his generosity and his care for her comfort: 'Mr Brydges is too kind to me to let me know the want of money.'

The running of the establishment at Canons was probably the easiest of the responsibilities that Cassandra assumed on her marriage. Mary Lake had been an affectionate and supportive wife and had moreover done her best to provide Brydges with a family, in particular with an heir to succeed to his family title and estates. Out of the nine children born to her, only two had survived – both boys – and therefore the more important to Brydges; so Cassandra was required to fill her predecessor's role both as a wife and a mother. Although she never had children of her own, she was nevertheless very fond and understanding of young people and seems to have been undeterred by the somewhat awkward nature of Brydges's two boys, John and Henry aged 8 and 5 respectively. At the time of their father's second marriage they had already started school at Isleworth near Sion Hill, and it was decided that they should continue there until they were ready to proceed to Westminster. John's health was not good, Henry was showing signs of being difficult, and they did not make as steady progress as Brydges expected, though their disappointing reports may have been due in part to their master's desire (based on financial considerations) to keep them with him as long as possible. Finally, in 1717, the boys were removed and sent to Westminster, each with his own manservant and footboy, and amply furnished with pocket money. During the holidays, educational journeys and visits to relatives were arranged for them and we hear of them with Brydges's cousins in Herefordshire, their aunts and cousins in Gloucestershire, Cassandra's brother at Wollaton and her half-brother at Wanstead.

Meanwhile Brydges and his wife were doing their share of entertaining in London, and preparing in a small way for the lavish hospitality that was to be a feature of life at Canons once the house was finished and Brydges had achieved his dukedom. Albemarle Street was conveniently placed for Westminster and St. James's, and not too far from the city, so that it was often a rendezvous for Brydges's political and business acquaintances. It was also the scene of card parties and formal dinners. Until work at Canons had been completed Brydges was reluctant for people to see it, apologising in letters for not keeping open house because of the disruption while construction and decorative work was going on. One can imagine the impatience with which he viewed progress or the lack of it on each of his visits, and the mounting irritation between him and his work force as he changed his mind about plans or cavilled at results that did not come up to his expectations. Although ultimately it was the magnificence of Canons that was to awe his contemporaries and leave a lasting impression, at the time of building Brydges was as much concerned with basic amenities and homely details as he was with embellishments. His insistence on having water-closets and bathrooms was a source of astonishment to his architects as well as to his workmen;

his concern with the prices and quality of raw materials they regarded as undue interference; his earnest desire to introduce a laboratory fitted for experiments and to have the morning sun coming into his bedroom and dressing room seemed indications of unusual tastes but ones to be indulged in so consequential a patron as their employer.

To Cassandra fell the task of keeping domestic arrangements running smoothly at both Albemarle Street and Canons. Equable in temperament, and essentially courteous and considerate in her dealing with everyone, she made a good employer and an efficient manager, setting high standards but always being reasonable in her demands. She made careful enquiries into their character and background before taking on any new servants and rarely made a bad choice; in fact, relatives and friends would write asking her to find servants for them or to recommend any who had been in her employ. Cassandra herself was firmly of the opinion that country girls and women gave more satisfactory service than those bred in the town, and she was especially keen to urge the merits of country-women as wet nurses. Brydges too saw an advantage in looking outside London for his servants. He consulted his brother-in-law, Theophilus Leigh of Adlestrop, when he wanted to appoint a new chaplain,[7] and his cousin Frances Brydges of Tyberton when he needed a coachman for journeys into the country: 'I should be glad to know if you've anyone in your eye that will be fit for us in the Country, for London Coachmen expect so much wages that I am loth to bring such a precedent into the Country.' To his sister Katherine Bourchier, in need of help over the running of her estate, he offered the services of his bailiff, 'a Gloucestershire man and very understanding in Country affairs.'

Although both came from a country background, Brydges adopted urban habits and tastes more quickly and completely than Cassandra, who – while adjusting to her husband's way of life, continued to prefer country pursuits and peaceful interludes for the enjoyment of reading, needlework, painting and music. Brydges became a hypochondriac in his later years, but as a young man he kept reasonably fit, his visits to Tunbridge Wells and Bath dictated more by fashion than by health needs. Cassandra, on the other hand, suffered considerably from ill-health, and while making light of this, was nevertheless driven to trying cures at the spas from time to time, with little success on the whole, although she did seem to benefit from the waters at Tunbridge Wells, or else from the comparative restfulness of visits there. The early years of their marriage, however, were spent almost entirely between the City and Edgware, and neither had many breaks from their demanding public life, such as Cassandra particularly would have liked. Brydges, tireless in pursuit of preferment, news of promising financial ventures or opportunities to add to his collection of books and pictures, spent much of his time in London with business and political acquaintances, but Cassandra was always in the background, ready to entertain at the house in Albemarle Street, or to accompany her husband to Canons on his visits of inspection, not particularly comfortable interludes while the house was being pulled down and remodelled.

The achievement of a dukedom was a milestone in Brydges's career in so far as it crowned his political and social ambitions and left him free to enjoy the prestige that the title brought and the kind of life that he thought fitting for one in his position. Cassandra was too level-headed to be influenced by the change in their circumstances and in any case was committed to supporting her husband along whatever ways his fortune carried him. Happily for her, in spite of revelling in his ducal role in public, Brydges could still be informal and completely relaxed with his friends in private; so Cassandra, who had greater sense of humour than her husband, no doubt smiled tolerantly when he (metaphorically) doffed his coronet, and was thankful for an opportunity to indulge in the domestic peace that suited *her* best.

CHAPTER 4

London Life and Friends.

To keep abreast of fashion and to be conveniently near Westminster and the Court of St. James's, the newly ennobled Chandos acquired another London dwelling in 1720, this time in St. James's Square where he took over Ormond House and gave it his own name instead. Along with the Earl of Southampton's development in Bloomsbury, St. James's Square had been an entirely new conception during the late 17th century, in that it was intended for aristocratic residents and planned as a complete unit, with a market, shops and inns in nearby secondary streets, and its own church. St. James's, Piccadilly, designed by Sir Christopher Wren in the 1670's was to serve this purpose, and Chandos already had a pew there.

During the 1720's, almost all the owners of the houses in the Square were peers with political and business interests, so Chandos had congenial neighbours. Their residences displayed varying degrees of elegance and modernity, according to how much attention and money could be spared from what was currently being lavished on out-of-town houses and country seats; but all were built of London-made, reddish-brown bricks (in accordance with the official regulations laid down after the disaster of the Great Fire) embellished in different styles, and incorporating particular features to suit individual tastes and needs. Portland stone was used for porches, window surrounds and hearths, and York stone for paving: English oak and Baltic pine for woodwork: plaster and ironwork to add decorative and individual details. And since for most owners the town house was merely an adjunct to a country dwelling – a seasonal pied-a-terre, an official base, a place for entertaining – the size and number of rooms was strictly functional, including a large dining room and salon, private apartments for the family, servants' quarters and perhaps a music room and library. Even in aristocratic developments such as St. James's and later squares tended to be, space was limited and the tall houses with long narrow areas behind to accommodate outhouses

St James's Square

and stables, had little in the way of gardens, whence stemmed the idea of having an open space in the centre of the development, laid out with trees and grass, to provide a pleasant outlook and somewhere for the residents to walk or sit in restful, shady surroundings. St. James's had a central lake, and according to a contemporary observer, it was 'the regularity of the buildings, the neatness of the pavement and the beauty of the bason in the middle' that gave the Square 'an appearance of grandeur equal to any other place in town.'[1]

At the same time as he was negotiating the purchase of Ormond House Chandos was committing himself to another aristocratic undertaking – the development of Cavendish Square. This had first been mooted in 1717 by Edward Harley who, as a result of his marriage to Henrietta Cavendish, heiress to the Duke of Newcastle, had acquired considerable property in the Marylebone area and was anxious to turn it to advantage. Among the first people to be approached as potential investors in the scheme were those who had been colleagues of Robert Harley his father, in the Tory ministry at the end of Anne's reign:

> The persons who propose to take ground for building in Marybone fields are Lord Dartmouth, Lord Caernaron, Lord Harcourt, Lord Bingley, Lord Bathurst, Lord Castleton. Those begining will in all probability build the whole ground, but measures must be taken for laying out the ground rents that there may be a beginning and present inclination may not be checked.[2]

Whereas in the case of the earlier squares, actual building had been left in the hands of speculative developers, Cavendish Square was architecturally designed and carried out, with great attention being paid to the achievement of symmetry and pleasing proportions in the final result. To quote Edward Harley again:

> I must begin with Cavendish Square which is my present mistress. I have been this day with Lord Castleton who had taken 72ft to the east of the Duke of Chandos's gardens. Lord Shelburne is to have as much or more next to him northwards. We have turned our thoughts how to make the best of the east side of the ground . . . . I think it will be very proper that the foundations of the church be laid this year and immediately begun. As to the market-house, I have taken me to direct . . . immediately the building. . . .

At the start, Chandos's ambitions as regards development on his own particular site were soaring – one huge mansion built on the same lines as

Canons, to equal the most prestigious town dwelling of any of his peers. However, this plan had to be modified in due course in favour of two small, separate houses, of which Chandos planned to use one himself while letting the other. The delays and setbacks which befell the Cavendish-Harley estate were in some degree due to the South Sea Bubble and reflected the extent to which notable politicians and business men were dependent on successful speculaton for the extra money to invest in building schemes. However, whether or not he was as much affected by the disaster as some of his peers, Chandos's diminishing concern with Cavendish Square was due not so much to lack of money as to the demands of a number of interests elsewhere. One feature of his plans, in respect of both St. James's and Cavendish Square, which remained unchanged, was his desire that people who lived there should have a reliable and safe supply of water, to which end he insisted that reservoirs should be included in the proposed layouts. Nor was this anxiety merely a consequence of his vested interest in the York Buildings Water Company that supplied the residential areas of London. Chandos was always concerned that his houses, whether in town or elsewhere, should have satisfactory plumbing and drainage, and hygienic water supplies.

During the periods he was in London, as opposed to those spent visiting his estates or fashionable spas, Chandos divided his time between Canons and St. James's Square. To cater for the needs of the family and guests, a skeleton staff was based in each residence while the Duke and Duchess took along with them personal servants, a secretary and footmen, the latter being specially chosen for their stamina, since an essential part of their duties was to run between the two dwellings with important messages. Both houses were adequately furnished but some plate and porcelain might be carried between the two to equip the dinner table on special occasions. Canons was the centre of the commissariat. Here supplies from Chandos's country estates were assembled and everyday needs catered for in the dairy, brewhouse, stillroom and kitchen; and from here went hampers of food to St. James's Square or further afield if the Duke and Duchess were at Tunbridge Wells or Bath. The gardens produced herbs and vegetables, the greenhouses melons and pineapples; fresh milk was supplied by the herd of Alderney cows that grazed in the park. From Herefordshire and Radnorshire came fruit, cider, bacon, cheese and fish; and at intervals, cattle and sheep were despatched by road to be slaughtered for meat at the end of their eight-day journey. Through his vested interests in the trading companies and his contacts abroad, Chandos was able to obtain exotic fruits and spices, wines, tea and coffee; and like others of his class he sent out and received countless presents – sophisticated luxuries and rarities from London and overseas being particularly acceptable to country cousins living at a distance, who could nevertheless respond with fish, game and venison – welcome additions to a town larder. Pots of lampreys from brother-in-law Edmund Chamberlayne were acknowledged by a gift of port and claret; a hare, two wood-cocks and a partridge from cousin Brydges of Tyberton, recompensed with 'a few Portugal onions, one dozen Sevil Oranges, ½ dozen Lemons, four China Oranges, and Citron water.'

The establishment at Canons was well staffed, workers being available to undertake most routine tasks about the house and grounds, as well as repairs to domestic equipment, garden tools, carriages, saddlery, etc. The Farmyard Table at mealtimes accommodated among others a farrier, a smith, a wheelwright, a shepherd, a cowherd and teamsters.[3] In the house, the Duchess had the help of female staff for keeping shelves and cupboards adequately stocked with preserves, cordials and sweetmeats. The confectionery room alone had '42 wainscot boxes and a wall-press for sweetmeats lyned with tyles'; the still-room must have been packed with the medicaments that the Duchess was always ready to offer to others as well as taking herself. Cassandra had learned about home-brewed remedies from Dr. Man, her brother's tutor, while she was living at Wollaton, where it was a family practice to dispense medicines to ailing servants and tenants;[4] and probably Chandos handed on to his wife some of the drugs and herbs that reached him via the ships belonging to the African Company, to be incorporated with other ingredients such as snail-water, orange flower water, rosemary and lavender tea. Laundry and mending were also done at Canons and clean linen dispensed from there. When engaging a new housekeeper, Cassandra was anxious that whoever was appointed should be able 'to wash and clear starch all the lace and cambrick which my Lord and I wear.' No doubt the standard of needlework in the house was high, for Cassandra was an enthusiastic and skilled needlewoman herself. While housekeeping at Wollaton she had helped to make good the damage done to upholstery and hangings by Parliamentary soldiers during the Civil Wars; now she turned her hand to making curtains, screens and bedhangings, and to keeping the household furnishings at Canons in good repair. Chandos was an admirer of his wife's artistry with her needle, as was Charles Gildon who eulogised it thus in his poem about

London Life and Friends

Canons, 'The Vision':

> Now with her ready needle paints the lawn,
> Where various figures are so finely drawn . . .
> Now with her fingers plies the gentle loom
> Then with her works adorns each spacious room . . .[5]

Although largely self-sufficient in basic necessities, Chandos's household did also call on the services of local workers at Edgware and in the city of London. During the 18th century London shops were coming into their own, offering a wide number of services and carrying an increasingly varied selection of goods which the shopkeepers were learning to display temptingly in their windows. For those with leisure and money, shopping became a social pastime, and while complaining of the fatigue involved in searching for a particular pattern of lace, or just the right material for a new gown or trimming for a bonnet, the ladies were in fact passing the time in a most agreeable and congenial manner. Nor were men proof against the dictates of fashion. Quite early on, Chandos had learned the importance of dressing fittingly and well, and this was a practice he continued throughout his life. The regular attendance that he and his wife put in at court also imposed on them a need for many new clothes. 'I intended to dine with his Grace yesterday which I did, in his new house in St. James's Square; his house is magnificently furnished and he and my Lady Duchess were very finely dressed having been at Court' reported Francis Brydges. So although plain sewing and mending were done in the house and an embroideress employed there for fancier stitching, the Duke and Duchess made use of London mantua-makers, tailors, shoe-makers, wig-makers, hatters and the like. There is no evidence that Cassandra was particularly interested in fashion, but her sense of fitness and of dignity would have ensured that she dressed suitably for her position and the occasion. When Letitia Cornwallis, Chandos's cousin, wrote to her from Tunbridge Wells describing an outrageous outfit worn by the Duchess of Hamilton, she assumed that Cassandra would be as shocked by the incident as she herself had been.

To acquire luxurious and unusual goods for himself and his household, Chandos made full use of his contacts abroad. Through them he obtained Persian carpets, Italian silk, taffeta and damask, Indian calico and muslin: mahogany and other hardwoods from Africa and the West Indies: porcelain from China: mirrors, snuff-boxes and clocks from France: musical instruments from Holland. But he also patronised English dealers to add to his collection of books, manuscripts and music:

to equip his writing-table: and to acquire the instruments that helped to furnish his library – a telescope, a microscope, a theodolite and an astronomical clock. Indeed, by the 1730's, London shops were importing a great number of goods that hitherto had been beyond the reach of the average buyer, so those who had in the past depended on foreign sources to fulfil their more exotic needs, could now satisfy themselves nearer home. Most mercers and haberdashers carried a full range of home-produced and foreign materials and their trade lists read almost like poetry – 'kerseymere, allapeens, dimities, duffels, muslins, sarsenets, flower'd and striped gauzes: fans, muffs, tippets and mittens'. Grocers and tea-merchants under the usual sign of three Sugar Loaves sold coffee, chocolate, 'cocoa-nutts', vermicelli, sago, starch, 'truffles with the best of all sorts of Grocery and Confectionery Wares'. Goldsmiths and toymen (thus did some silver-smiths style themselves) offered jewellery, candlesticks, toothpicks, watches; and cabinet-makers – 'chairs either covered, matted or caned, sconces, pier and chimney-glasses, and blinds for windows made and curiously painted on canvas, silk or wire.'

Both Chandos and his wife were hospitable. They had been accustomed to visiting relatives from an early age and to receiving visits in return, and while living at Wollaton, Cassandra and her brother had entertained friends and neighbours very frequently, and delighted in filling the house with guests on particular occasions such as birthdays and Christmas. Much of Chandos's entertaining now had to be the formal reception of important figures in politics and business, or notable visitors from abroad. On these occasions protocol prevailed, and especially at Canons the grandeur and rigid conventionality involved must have turned the proceedings into a marathon of endurance. Guests and servants alike were expected to abide by the rules of the household, strictly observing times of meals, precedence as regards places at table, or which of the state rooms were accessible and when. Even going to services in the private chapel or at the parish church of St. Lawrence, Whitchurch, meant a ceremonial progress between lines of servants, together with the Duke's Chelsea pensioners, whose other duties included guarding the entrance gates and patrolling the grounds at night. Military precision and efficiency were indeed key factors in the household management at Canons, perhaps because ultimate executive responsibility was in the hands of the Steward, Colonel Watkins, himself an ex-soldier.

There was certainly plenty to interest guests at Canons when they were not being entertained by the Duke personally. The house itself was a

London Life and Friends

work of art, filled with paintings, carvings and pieces of sculpture, ornate furniture and elaborate decoration. The grounds were vast, with terraces and formal gardens adorned with statues and leaden vases in the vicinity of the house: a lake, parkland and shady walks beyond. Here, exotic birds – storks, macaws and flamingoes – could be seen, along with deer and cattle. Also open to view were the kitchen garden, the greenhouses – heated by turf specially imported from Holland, and the cucumber and melon frames shrouded in oiled paper 'affording more serviceable heat and preventing that scorching which happens through glass.' During the evening and at services in the chapel, the 'Canons Musick' performed under the direction of Dr. Pepusch. The group consisted of between sixteen and twenty-four players of wood-wind, string instruments and drums, who could also act as a choir, performing a wide repertoire of music. This included works by Haym, Purcell, Blow, Lully and Vivaldi, together with those specially composed by Handel for Chandos who had made the acquaintance of the composer at the Hanoverian court and been among the first to encourage and employ him when he came to England.

On less formal occasions when the guests were relatives or close friends, the atmosphere tended to be relaxed and the entertainments quite homely: games of cards, chess or backgammon, conversation or smoking a pipe with Chandos who obtained his own favourite tobacco from Gambia through the African Company. At such times the main meal might be served earlier – between 3 and 4 o'clock, when Chandos had served 'a little broath, and a piece of roast mutton, and a couple of chickens and some peas;' and certainly the guests were not aware of being caught up in the elaborate machinery that operated on state occasions. In fact we learn from their correspondence, it was during these visits that members of the Chandos circle hoped to catch the ear of the Duke and engage his sympathy or support for some personal project. William Brydges, Chandos's cousin, gives us this description of one such occasion:

> Upon Saturday last, my nephew and I did goe to Cannons, where we were kindly received and generously entertained. I never saw so much grandeur and order in any family. Nothing was irksome but late hours. Between 11 and 12 we went to Chapell. About 2 of the clock we were sent for to his Lordship in his Library, staid there till Dinner (which was about an hour) and after Dinner were entertained with ingenious conversation, generous wine and a pipe will

between 9 and 10. Then went to supper. After supper we drank two or three glasses of wine whilst the Musicall Instruments were tuned and then we were entertained with a Concert for an hour or more, then took a glass of wine and a pipe and soe to Bed, and by this time 'twas between 1 and 2 of the clock.[6]

When in London, the Duke and his wife could resort to outside entertainments to divert their guests if domestic pleasures seemed inadequate. Whether, as he grew older or less frenzied in pursuit of useful contacts, Chandos stayed long enough at the theatre to see a play through to the end, we do not know, but he regularly received and paid for playbills from the playhouses at Covent Garden, Drury Lane and the Haymarket. Although performances met with very mixed receptions and sometimes ended with members of the audience doing harm to the actors, each other and the building itself, nevertheless playgoing was a fashionable pursuit, and visitors to London would have appreciated the opportunity of thus participating in the social life of the capital. Both in their letters and personal expense accounts, Chandos's nephews William and Thomas Leigh record having seen plays and heard operas and oratorios at Covent Garden and Drury Lane; and this letter from Cassandra to William Brydges indicates that she and her husband had 'season' tickets that they lent to visitors:

In hopes the two Inclosed Tickets for the Opera may prove an agreeable divertion for your Spare Hours in town, I take the liberty of sending them to you, and desiring you will please to use them while you stay in London; and when you return to the country, to be so good to send them again to me.

Mention of the opera is a reminder that Chandos was one of the first patrons in London of this new form of entertainment, his enthusiasm for it no doubt inspired by his own Master of Music, Handel, who was largely responsible for its introduction into England. Because considerable expenses were involved – for the engagement of Italian singers and elaborate staging – opera was very much a pursuit of the wealthy. When the Royal Academy of Music was formed in 1719 expressly to promote the art of operatic singing, the King headed the subscription list with £1,000, and three lords, Chandos, Burlington and Newcastle, followed suit with the same amount, continuing faithful in their efforts to support the venture – unlike George I who rather speedily lost interest in it.

But at this juncture opera was not a lasting success in England, partly because it involved foreign performers and only appealed to rather

London Life and Friends

cultivated tastes: also because it was essentially an aristocratic fashion and the factiousness of its supporters in other spheres – politics and court intrigues for instance – began to be reflected within the Academy and between the composers and singers favoured by its members. By 1737, all operatic productions had ceased, but music had now become an accepted accompaniment of theatrical performances and indeed of many social gatherings. Each of the three playhouses had its own musicians who provided musical interludes and sometimes gave concerts in their own right. Members of the royal family and the aristocracy arranged private entertainments, and music was available to the public in the pleasure gardens at Ranelagh, Vauxhall and Marylebone.

Although the music was undoubtedly a major attraction, it was not the only reason for frequenting the parks and gardens. For public figures like Chandos and his friends, these were places for seeing and being seen. During the daytime it was a socially acceptable pursuit to stroll along the tree-lined paths of St. James's Park or Marylebone Gardens observing the company, greeting friends, and no doubt keeping oneself informed of the latest fashions. In the evenings, there would be concerts, masquerades, firework displays and private supper parties at Ranelagh and Vauxhall, and when not themselves entertaining, the Duke and Duchess would give away tickets to their friends. 'My Lord has ordered three tickets for the Masquerade to be sent to your Ladyship as soon as they are given out. I hope the entertainment will be as fine as you can expect,' ran a letter from Cassandra to Lady Buck. The other daytime meeting places for the men were the coffee-houses, many of which, by the 1720's were becoming more like clubs, so regular was the clientele that frequented them and so homogeneous their interests and inclinations. Political opinion, business interests, artistic or literary pursuits all characterised particular houses and determined their attraction, for conversation was the first objective of their patrons; after which came the opportunity to play cards, to read the current newspapers, hear the latest news from home and abroad, and often to conclude business deals. Even though anyone of Chandos's standing would subscribe to papers for reading at home, nevertheless other people's interpretation of the news, rumours and even conjectures could prove useful in determining future moves and decisions.

As has been said, much of the entertaining done at Canons and St. James's Square was official, in that the guests had political or social significance, rather than being personal friends. In her letters Cassandra mentions that Indian princes, the Kings of Denmark and of Prussia were among the visitors to Canons; and in London, Chandos on various occasions entertained the Prince of Wales, the Duke of Grafton, Speaker Onslow and Lord Carteret. Sir Robert Walpole, though prominent in politics, was regarded as a personal friend. Cassandra's offers, acceptance or rejection of invitations are clues to other members of their circle of friends. Lady Coventry, the Countess of Suffolk, the Duchess of Marlborough and her daughter the Duchess of Montagu were among those whom Cassandra met at court and who, like herself, were also regular visitors to Tunbridge Wells and Bath. With the Drummonds, their neighbours at Edgware, they were on easy visiting terms, dropping in on each other to discuss family news and look round the grounds of their respective residences, the Drummonds' summer house situated on a hill being visible from one of the avenues that crossed the park at Canons, or alternatively, Chandos's palatial dwelling seen to advantage from the summer-house.

Lord Bathurst, Lord Harcourt, Edward Harley (2nd Lord Oxford), Lord Bingley, the Duke of Shrewsbury and Lord Burlington had all been active in politics before this, some of them colleagues of Brydges while he was Paymaster during the last years of Anne's reign. In the 1720's however, it was not politics but a shared interest in architecture, art and collecting that drew all these together socially. Harcourt, Bingley, Bathurst and Chandos were parties to the Cavendish Square development at much the same time as Burlington was transforming his own house in Piccadilly and laying out the streets behind it. All these too were builders or improvers of country houses that had claims to fashion and fame – Bathurst at Cirencester, Shrewsbury at Heythrop, Harcourt at Nuneham Courtenay, Harley at Wimpole and Welbeck (his wife's properties) and Bingley at Bramham. Another member of this circle was Sir Richard Child, later Lord Castlemain, Cassandra's half-brother, who had raised a huge Palladian mansion on the site of his father's old-fashioned seat at Wanstead, and lived and entertained there on a lavish scale. Like Canons, the house was a mecca for sight-seeing visitors from London; and like Canons also it became famed for its hospitality, parties ranging from intimate family gatherings to magnificent balls, entertainments for the tenants and employees on the estate, and assemblies which afforded a variety of diversions including card-games, dancing and music.

Hospitality, either formal or informal was regularly exchanged within this aristocratic circle; and so, it must be supposed, were views on building and the work of the various craftsmen needed to achieve the effects desired by these connoisseurs. As we shall see, there was a clearly

Ranelagh Gardens

Conversation Piece at Wanstead

defined circuit within which moved architects and craftsmen such as plasterers, carpenters, carvers, iron-workers etc all helped along by personal recommendations from their employers, who also gave advice and suggestions to each other. Lord Bingley, probably his own architect during the building of Bramham, offered his opinions to Chandos on the improvements being made at Canons. Lord Bathurst inspected the houses of his friends as well as asking for the latter's advice before embarking on a new layout for his mansion and estate at Cirencester. Lord Burlington, as a result of his own passion for the subject, established himself as the leading judge of excellence in architecture. Thus the new ideas embodied in publications such as Campbell's *Vitruvius Britannicus,* Palladio's books on architecture, and Switzer's on gardening, and being tried out by individuals, dominated conversation and were taken as seriously as political issues had been when Chandos and his friends were actively engaged in government.

The poet Alexander Pope, a close personal friend of Lord Bathurst, was an outspoken critic of extravagance in building ('I curse such lavish cost and little skill') and himself an exponent in the design of his villa at Twickenham of the trends in architecture and landscaping that he approved of. In his two poems, addressed to Lord Bathurst and Lord Burlington, he described contemporary trends in taste, acknowledged the influence that leaders in these might have, and stressed the need for this influence to be exercised to good effect. He had no time for the wealthy man who identified excellence with expense and lacked 'good sense which only is the gift of Heaven'; and who, having impoverished himself in pursuit of showy effects would nevertheless be 'proud to catch cold at a Venetian door' and 'starve by rules of art.' Whether 'gracious Chandos . . . beloved at sight', or the portrait of the lord with majestic mien who presided over Timon's villa most nearly reflected Pope's true opinion of Chandos is uncertain, but his approval of Bathurst and Burlington was definitely unreserved, the former 'yet unspoiled by wealth', and having 'the sense to value riches, with the art to enjoy them'; the latter, making falling arts his care, was praised for erecting new wonders and repairing the old: 'These are imperial works and worthy kings.'

CHAPTER 5

Family Responsibilities

Much as he enjoyed his ducal role and the active social life it entailed, Chandos was at heart a family man with a lively sense of responsibility where his relations and dependants were concerned, and unlimited generosity towards cases of need that were brought to his notice.

Being the only two of Mary Lake's children to survive, the boys, John (born 1705) and Henry (born 1708) were particularly important to their father who was typical of his class in wanting to perpetuate his family and ensure the uninterrupted line of succession to his titles and estates. Thus while the boys were still in his charge it was an over-riding concern that they should receive a sound education, have opportunities of making the right friends and be married advantageously. After school at Westminster, John was sent to Oxford in 1719 to finish his academic training, not to New College where his father had been, but to Balliol which had sheltered his Brydges cousins. Chandos allowed him £400 a year to meet personal expenses and pay for his food and lodging in college; and he had a servant, a footman, a groom and three horses for his own use. Although quite law-abiding while he himself was at Oxford, Chandos seems to have feared that circumstances were changing and not necessarily for the better. His son was a Gentleman-Commoner, as he had been, paying double fees for the honour of sharing the meals of the Fellows at High Table, yet in this connection Chandos was driven to comment:

> In my time, wee alwaise did so at the table with the vice-Warden (when the Head of the House was not there) and the Senior Fellow. I cannot approve the new fashion I hear is coming up of the noblemen's keeping table in their own chambers.

And Duchess Cassandra in one of her letters to John felt obliged to remind him:

> Considering how short time you have to stay at the University, my Lord would by no means have you lye out of it or indeed go a-visiting from it.

Even an invitation to stay with the Marlboroughs at Blenheim must be declined. Clearly it was feared that John might very easily be distracted and deflected from his studies.

In 1721, after leaving Oxford, Lord Caernarvon (John had assumed this title when his father became a duke) was sent abroad to make some acquaintance with foreign languages and countries, and to widen his social experience; and for two years in charge of a tutor he travelled through Holland, France, Italy and Germany. He had letters of introduction to friends of his father in Leyden, Paris, Rome and at the court of Hanover – contacts that it was hoped might prove advantageous to him later on. Meanwhile at home, Chandos was endeavouring to arrange a suitable marriage for his son – 'suitable' implying that the lady should be an heiress or at least well-dowered, and young enough to produce an heir to the Brydges' titles and estates. After several had been considered and turned down, Catherine Tollemache, daughter of the Earl of Dysart, was selected, wealthy certainly but twenty years older than her intended husband. This was the bride that Caernarvon was expected to accept; although it was unlikely that Chandos would have forced the issue against the unwillingness of either party, it was fortunate that both were agreable to the marriage, which took place at Lord Dysart's house in Arlington Street in September 1724. Then 'Lord and Lady Dysart brought the bride and bridegroom home to Canons where, and at London, they lived with us for two years', recorded the Duchess.

At the same time as he was seeking a bride for his son, Chandos was also taking steps to obtain a seat in Parliament for him, by purchasing properties in Steyning, Sussex, which carried enough votes to ensure his success at election time. He also arranged that his own Clerkship of the Hanaper should revert to John, so that the young man took a step into public life as well as into marriage. The birth of his first child Catherine in December 1725 was something of a disappointment to the grandfather; 'We should have liked a grandson but a daughter is a very acceptable New Year's gift'; however, John was young and his wife still capable of having more children. In 1726 the Caernarvons acquired a house of their own in Arlington Street and it was here that John fell ill in April 1727. In spite of his symptoms, small-pox was not suspected at first because he was believed to have had the disease while he was travelling abroad; and by the time it was diagnosed he was seriously ill. His pregnant wife and small daughter took refuge at Canons, where Chandos also remained, while the Duchess who had had smallpox and was not afraid of it, stayed in London to nurse her stepson. Her efforts were in vain though, and John died, shortly before the birth of his second daughter Jane.

The unexpected death of Caernarvon and his failure to produce a male heir now switched Chandos's attention and hopes to his younger son Henry. Though not unintelligent, the latter had been an unwilling and unruly scholar and failed to settle down even when he went up to college at Cambridge. His propensity for spending money and for reckless riding was a continual source of concern to his step-mother, and failed to impress his uncle Theophilus Leigh who commented: 'Fine feathers make fine birds. Riding the great Horse and Dancing may make him a Beau but I doubt will conduce little to making his fortune in the world.'[1] After six months it was decided that his time might be better spent abroad; he was sent to Leyden to study but had to be summoned home hastily from there when his brother died. The subsequent birth of John's second daughter meant that the title of Lord Caernarvon and role of heir now passed to Henry, and made it vital that a marriage should be arranged for him as soon as possible. Chandos' choice of a bride fell on Mary Bruce, daughter of Lord Bruce and grand-daughter of Lord Ailesbury, an exiled supporter of the Stuarts and a friend of the Brydges and Leigh families with whom he corresponded regularly. The marriage took place in December 1728 and the birth of a son James (Lord Wilton) to Henry and his wife in 1731 relieved Chandos of immediate fears for the future so far as the family name was concerned.

Over Henry's own future, some doubts still hung. Marriage had not made him any less extravagant or unreliable, and despite living in his father's houses and at his father's expense, he was continually in debt, yet it was high time that he should give some thought to his family and assume some public responsibility commensurate with his position. Without much willingness or assiduity on his part, but thanks to the efforts of his father, he was made in turn First Lord of the Bedchamber, Master of Horse and Groom of the Stole to the Prince of Wales, but primarily in 1728 he was prevailed on to offer himself as a Parliamentary candidate for Hereford, Chandos's old seat. His father's reasons for urging him into this role are somewhat surprising and do not inspire confidence in the character of the young men who graced the House of Commons at this time:

FAMILY OF HENRY BRYDGES

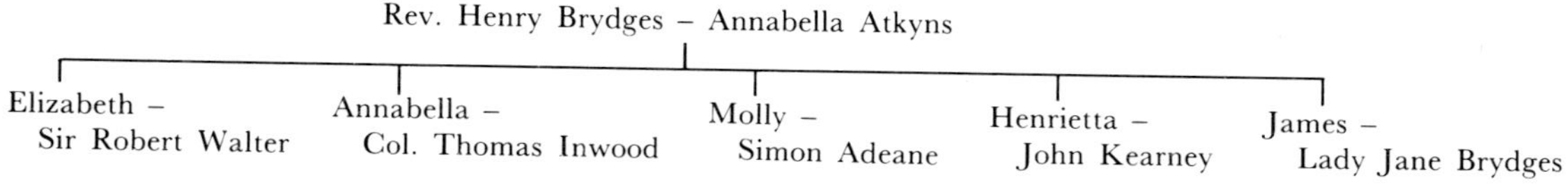

Rev. Henry Brydges – Annabella Atkyns

- Elizabeth – Sir Robert Walter
- Annabella – Col. Thomas Inwood
- Molly – Simon Adeane
- Henrietta – John Kearney
- James – Lady Jane Brydges

FAMILY OF MARY BRYDGES

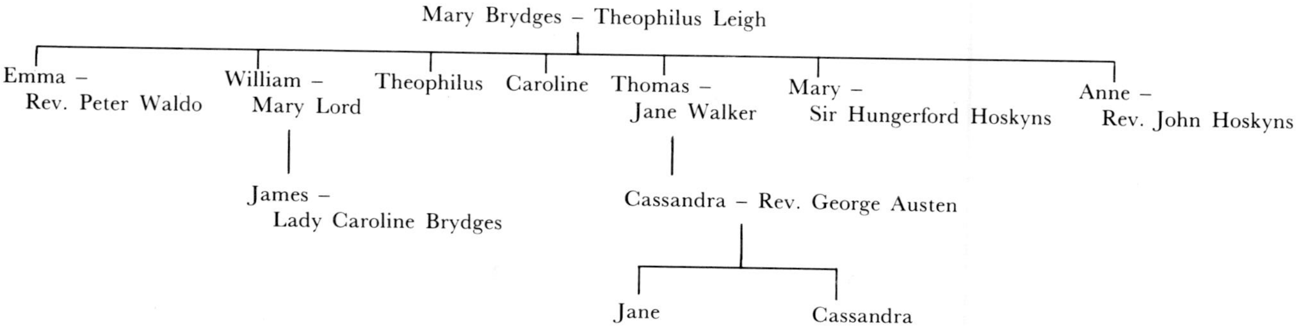

Mary Brydges – Theophilus Leigh

- Emma – Rev. Peter Waldo
- William – Mary Lord
- Theophilus
- Caroline
- Thomas – Jane Walker
- Mary – Sir Hungerford Hoskyns
- Anne – Rev. John Hoskyns

James – Lady Caroline Brydges

Cassandra – Rev. George Austen
- Jane
- Cassandra

> Lord Caernarvon is a young man whom I would be very glad to have in Parliament in hopes to give him thereby an early turn to Business and prevent his running into the Vices of the Town which Men of Age and Quality when they have nothing else to do, are apt to be tainted with.[2]

Nor were the measures taken to ensure Caernarvon's election any more praiseworthy. The burgesses of Hereford were persuaded to vote for him by means of gifts and lavish hospitality, 'more substantial arguements than Prayers or Requests'. Chandos justified these efforts in a letter to Francis Brydges that is difficult to reconcile with the above statement and rings somewhat hollowly in view of his own contribution to such practices in the past:

> I confess very frankly to you it goes against me to take such a Course as this, which a man of the least understanding in the world must foresee will be the ruin of his Country. But all the Corporations in England as well as almost all sorts and Ranks of people are really infected with such an infamous degree of Corruption that there is hardly a possibility of getting into Parliament without it, and therefore I comfort myself with the thoughts that I do it for a contrary purpose from what most do, to bring in one who will have no view of Profit to himself by it, but who will be always Zealous to support the true interest to his Country and at the same time not be wanting in his Duty to his Prince.[3]

What made the whole business even more questionable was that Caernarvon was still several months under age for membership of Parliament. Chandos knew this but argued: 'He will be pretty near of age when Parliament meets and besides it will be impossible for any to prove he is not of age already.' However, he was over-confident. A petition was drawn up demanding another election, and it cost £700 to have this' suppressed and Caernarvon's membership confirmed. Altogether very considerable and unlooked-for expense had been incurred – £2,500 to be exact; and Chandos must have wondered whether it had been worth while when he found son most reluctant to go down to Hereford to thank his supporters and subsequently to show some commitment to their affairs. Whether because of this, or for other reasons, Chandos began to lose interest in his properties in the city of Hereford at this point, and when his son next offered himself for election in 1732, it was for his brother's constituency at Steyning where it was reckoned that the necessary votes could be secured for about one third the price of those at Hereford.

In addition to launching his sons into careers and matrimony, Chandos had meanwhile been furthering the interest of his brothers and sisters. Nor was this concern confined to his own generation. His parents, as well as offering hospitality to a host of young relatives, had also helped to promote their marriage prospects as they grew up. So after the death of Lord Chandos in 1714 and Lady Chandos in 1719, the young Chandos and his wife assumed their practice of keeping open house for members of the family, being especially welcoming to the younger generation on whose behalf they were prepared to take endless pains to secure suitable marriage partners and worthwhile settlements. Of Chandos's own immediate family, Frank who died in 1714 had enjoyed the fruits of several offices obtained through his brother's influence – Cashier to the Commissioners for Salt Duties, Receiver-General of duties on malt, and Comptroller of Customs at Newcastle-under-Lyme. Henry, who went into the church, also received a series of promotions thanks to his brother's efforts. His first appointment was to the living of Broadwell in Gloucestershire (obtained through Theophilus Leigh) and then in turn he became Archdeacon and Prebendary of Rochester, Chaplain to George I and a Canon of St. Paul's Cathedral. Henry frequently officiated at the marriages of members of his family, and his advice was sought and valued. It was while he was at Broadwell that he met and married Annabella Atkyns, niece of Robert Atkyns the Gloucestershire historian, whose family had wide estates in the county. In due course Henry's children were helped into favourable marriages by Chandos – Elizabeth to Sir Robert Walter of Sarsden, Annabella to Colonel Thomas Inwood, Molly to Simon Adeane, Henrietta to John Kearney, and James to his own cousin, Chandos's grand-daughter Lady Jane Brydges. All these marriages were arranged with scrupulous attention to detail in the interests of the parties concerned and of their families. Weeks passed while letters were exchanged, legal points clarified and all possible loopholes closed. In the case of Annabella, Chandos was at last able to report:

> I am just come down Stairs from the Dining Room where I have seen the Ceremony performed of marriage between Colonel Inwood and my Niece; they dine with us and then go down to Stanmore, my sister Brydges going along with them. Tomorrow they dine at Cannons.

Careful manoeuvring had ensured £10,000 in investments for the couple, 'so that they have coming in about £1000 a year besides his Commission in the Guards'; and in addition Chandos had given his niece 40 shares in the Sun Fire Company 'for her separate use and Pin Money'. Arrangements were also made for allowances to go to any children of the marriage, as well as an income to Annabella should she be widowed.

Chandos's eldest sister Mary married Theophilus Leigh of Adlestrop, Gloucestershire, a close and much respected friend of the Brydges family. Mary died quite early in 1703, and possibly this fact increased her brother's feeling of responsibility in respect of her children. In turn her daughters were invited to Canons, entertained, betrothed and married in the chapel there – Emma to the Rev. Peter Waldo, Mary to Sir Hungerford Hoskyns (a Herefordshire neighbour of the Brydges) and Ann to his brother the Rev. John Hoskyns. Cassandra, a rebel, refused to accept the gentleman found for her by Chandos and instead got herself engaged to Captain Thomas Wight her cousin. Mary's eldest son James took up a career in the army thanks to his uncle who obtained a commission for him in 1711, writing on this occasion to the Duke of Argyle:

> Her Majesty having been pleased to give leave to Colonel Ansell to resign his post of Lieutenant Colonell in Sir Robert Rich's Regiment to a nephew of mine Captain Leigh by which he'll have the Honour to serve under your Grace's command, I humbly beg leave to trouble you with this, to introduce him to kiss your Hands and to recommend him to your Protection; I would not take the liberty to say anything in his behalf if I was not persuaded He'll make it his great study to merit the Patronage and interest your Grace out of your Generosity will be pleas'd to afford him, and which I am confident will make so deep an Impression of Gratitude in his mind as no time will efface.[4]

Regrettably, James did not fulfil these expectations. While in Portugal he complained continually in letters to his father – of the hilliness of the streets in Lisbon, the lack of tents, uniforms and arms, and not having enough to do; and on his return, got involved in a quarrel with one of his subordinates which ended in a duel. James died before reaching his majority and it was through Mary's second son William that the family lands descended to his son James who strengthened the tie with the Brydges by marrying Chandos's grand-daughter Caroline. Mary's third son Theophilus became Master of Balliol College, Oxford, and carried on

The Hon. Mary Leigh

Brereton Bourchier

Family Responsibilities

his father's role (after the latter's death in 1725) of being a confidant for all the family. Chandos turned to him for help in composing memorial inscriptions for the tombs of his second wife, and of his daughter-in-law, Lady Caernarvon. It is interesting to note from the letters they exchanged over these in 1735 and 1738 that Chandos had not lost his command of Latin. The fourth son, the Rev. Thomas, married Jane Walker and their daughter Cassandra became the mother of Jane Austen.

Chandos's second sister Elizabeth, who married first Alexander Jacob, and then the Rev. Thomas Dawson, was a continual source of worry and of irritation to Chandos and his wife. She was clearly a difficult discontented person, always sorry for herself and expectant that other people should rally round to support her. Her second husband deserted her in order to do better for himself, so that she was obliged to fall back upon the charity of her family. Chandos allowed her an annuity and paid off her debts at intervals; Duchess Cassandra gave her extra sums of money to meet particular crises. Her two sons also were befriended by Chandos. For Alexander Jacob 'my lord bought a levetenant-collonell's commission in my Lord Hinchinbroke's regiment and upon a quarrell with his collonell the year after in which he did not behave himself well, he was forced to sell his commission'. Meanwhile his younger brother Robert had tried and rejected as uncongenial, three posts found for him by Chandos with the Turkey Company, the African Company and a development in Nova Scotia.

Of the three remaining sisters, Anne married into the legal family of the Walcots, neighbours and friends of the Brydges in Herefordshire, while a match was arranged for Emma with Edmund Chamberlayne of Maugersbury to whom she remained patiently faithful in spite of his exceptional meanness and lack of family affection.[5] Lastly there was Katherine, wife of Brereton Bourchier of Barnsley, much loved and trusted by her mother and her brother, and so satisfactorily matched that, like Chandos, she dispensed hospitality, help and comfort to other members of the family rather than asking these for herself. Her house was used as a stopping-place by those journeying between London or Herefordshire and Bath, and like her parents she took in children while their mothers were ill or pregnant, and stood as a godmother to innumerable nephews and nieces.

Brereton Bourchier died in 1713 and immediately Chandos rallied round with offers of help to his sister in the management of her estate and an invitation to make an unlimited stay with him: 'My wife desires me to assure you, you'll be heartily welcome; and if there is no business can make you think of living in Gloucestershire, you shall bear no expense with us.' However, Katherine had character and determination, and politely but firmly insisted on managing her affairs herself. In due course her daughter Martha showed the same kind of independence. As a child she was much approved of by Chandos, who wrote to his sister:

> My giving you the trouble of this is to return you many thanks for my niece Bourchier's good company. She is with us at Cannons and indeed I cannot but congratulate you upon so deserving a daughter whose good qualities are so visible that you have all the reason in the world to expect she'll prove a real blessing and comfort to you. I hope you intend to let her have the remainder of her education with us.[5]

Naturally, Martha's uncle felt it incumbent upon him to find a husband for his niece but in spite of the trouble taken over this, she turned down two highly promising and willing suitors. As this seemed out of character, an explanation was sought – and found, in her infatuation with her cousin Alexander Jacob. Chandos felt that Alexander's mother was largely to blame for putting ideas into Martha's head and taking every opportunity to throw the two young people together.

> My sister Jacob said . . . that she (Martha) was in love with either her Cousin Leigh or her son, and I leave it to you to judge whether it was a fitting thought to put into the head of a young Creature of a man she could not avoid seeing every now and then: and whether my sister could say such a thing as that without having, according to her simple cunning, some design in it.[6]

All the same, in view of his strong disapproval of the situation and 'to avoid the imputation of the world believing she engaged her affections in such a manner while she was under my roof', Chandos arranged for Martha to return to her mother at Barnsley.

> All I proposed in desiring her Company was to see her happily married and since she has positively refused hearkening to the match I had provided for her, I don't know any advantage she can reap here with us. I'll send my coach down with her on Monday next or Wednesday sevennight according as by your answer to this I shall find it will be more convenient for you.[7]

In spite of his own mingled disappointment and anger, Chandos

Family Responsibilities

counselled his sister not to be too hard on her daughter, and Cassandra – clearly very much in sympathy with the girl – wrote to her consolingly.

In due course, Alexander Jacob went abroad with his regiment and Martha reconciled herself to marriage with Henry Perrot of North Leigh, Oxon, a regular visitor to Canons and one of the Chandos circle of connoisseurs. Of this arrangement, Cassandra wrote to Emma Chamberlayne:

> I heartily wish my cousin Bourchier all imaginable happiness in the match now in treaty for her. Mr. Perrot's character is so very good that we have no reason to doubt of it.

However it would appear that 'all happiness' was not to be Martha's lot. She and her husband did not get on well, and after a while they separated, at which point the sympathies of Chandos and his wife veered away from Martha towards her husband, who continued to be a frequent visitor to Canons and Shaw Hall, and corresponded regularly with Chandos on personal and business matters. He played an important part in arranging the marriage between Annabella Brydges and Colonel Inwood, and assisted also in the transference of Annabella's mother's estate to Lord Bathurst. Martha meanwhile became increasingly difficult and unco-operative as she moved about with her two daughters Martha and Cassandra between London, Bath and a house 'within two miles of Barnsley'.

At the time of her marriage to James Brydges, Cassandra Willoughby automatically took over a share of responsibility for members of her husband's family, and the contents of her letter-books are proof of how conscientiously she kept in touch with them, and concerned herself with their circumstances, enquiring after their health, prescribing for their ailments and supplying financial help when necessary. Chandos reciprocated with an interest in Cassandra's family, who although they welcomed his friendship, were never in need of material assistance. Francis and Rothwell Willoughby, nephews, were regular visitors to Canons, as was Cassandra's mother; and there were frequent exchanges of hospitality with the Child family at Wanstead. Sir Richard was pleased to have Chandos as a godfather for his son in 1711:

> My little son we design to make a Christian this week and your assistance towards it will be a very great favour and if you will honour us so much. I must leave it to you to chuse Friday or Saturday evening, either will be equal to us.

And a few years later in 1717, Chandos was instrumental in obtaining a title for Child:

> According to your desire the Night before you went out of Town, I have wrote to Lord Lansdown (without naming your name) to know if he had any objection to a relation of mine's taking the title of Bath, the King being graciously pleas'd to intend to bestow a Title of Peerage upon him. I find by his answer that he has, and that he looks upon that title as belonging to his family. . . . I thought it proper to give you this notice that you might let me know what other title you'd choose, and the sooner I receive your answer the better, in regard I believe I could prevail to have the Warrant signed.[10]

Falmouth or Maldon were suggested, but in the end Viscount Castlemain was the name chosen.

While habitually deferring to her husband's wishes, Duchess Cassandra also took the initiative on occasion, in furthering the interests of her own relatives. It is evident from her writings that she held members of her family in an affection that went further than periodic present-giving and the exchange of letters of conventional greetings. Through the years of their childhood and education, she followed the progress of her brothers' and half-brothers' children with sincere concern but never undue interference. Thus both at Wollaton and at Wanstead, she was a welcome visitor whose companionship was appreciated by parents and children alike. When it seemed desirable she gave advice or dispensed information, and like her husband she acted as a go-between on occasion. For instance, on behalf of a Cornwallis cousin, she approached the Countess of Derby in 1717:

> Knowing you to be very good, I can't doubt of a pardon for a liberty I am going to take in behalf of a relation of mine who now stands in the room of Lord Winchester for the County of Carmarthen; he has not the honour to be acquainted either with Lord Ashburnham or Lord Anglesey who both have many votes at their command in the county. Would your Ladyship be so obliging as to represent Mr. Cornwallis to them as a person of merit, I believe it might influence them to write to their agents there in his behalf, and I have to assure your Ladyship that he is of such honest principles as will make you pleased with the good offices you do him.

And for her nephew, she wrote in 1720 to Dr. Hyloff in Cambridge:

My nephew, Thomas Willloughby standing one of the candidates for the election for the University, occasioned me to solicit your vote and interest for him. I could not desire your favour for him of you upon any other account than that of his being nephew to my Aunt Wendy whose memory I believe will induce you to be serviceable to one that was so nearly related to her; and therefore for her sake it is that I make this request to you. . . .

This reference to Lettice Wendy reflects Cassandra's own affection for the aunt who befriended her and her brothers after their mother's marriage to Sir Josiah Child, and whose judgment, kindness and piety she greatly admired.

As usual with members of their class, the 'family' of the Duke and Duchess comprised considerably more than their immediate relatives, since it extended to their numerous godchildren, those drawn into their circle by marriage, members of their household staff, and the needy whom they befriended. Regularly each year, married couples added to their families, so there was an almost uninterrupted series of christenings to be attended, where members of the family always appeared among the godparents, along with close friends and notable acquaintances. (The Prince of Wales stood godfather to Henry Brydges's daughter Caroline). Both the Duke and Duchess took seriously their responsibilities as godparents, sending gifts to midwives, nurses and whoever officiated at the christening services, thereafter continuing to mark birthdays and other landmarks in the careers of the children concerned. Chandos and his wife were devout people and this is reflected in the way they carried out their responsibilities in respect of their godchildren. Both also had a caring attitude to their servants. Although Chandos could be extremely impatient and irritable with the craftsmen he employed in his various building projects, he seems to have been more equable where his domestic staff were concerned. Of course, there were strict household rules that defined in detail the duties of every particular servant, and provided they observed these, there was no reason why they should have got into trouble. All were paid well, especially those who worked in the front of the house and came into contact with visitors, for although Chandos himself habitually dispensed largesse wherever he went, he nevertheless thought it wrong that servants should be dependent on tips, even in a small way.

Chandos was generous too in his willingness to promote members of his household who showed promise. There was competition to get into the choir and the orchestra at Canons since this might lead to further opportunities. The high standards maintained in singing and playing involved strict training, hard work and considerable versatility as the performers were required to undertake jobs about the house when not actively engaged in making music. But any particular skills or willingness to serve were noticed and acknowledged – as in the case of Ghiraldo, a valet-violinist who was sent abroad with Lord Caernarvon: 'he shaves very well and hath an excellent hand on the violin and all necessary languages'. Thomas Jones, 'who has a very good hand upon the Harp,' during one of Chandos's visits to Shaw, was given leave to go to Oxford 'to pick up a little money there' and put under the protection of Henry Perrot.

> I take it for granted you'll have a great many of your acquaintance with you on this occasion; if you'll be so kind to recommend him and countenance him with your Protection it will be a great act of goodness in you to the poor Fellow.

George Munroe, who entered the house as a page 'hath been so successful in his improvement under Mr. Handel and Dr. Pepusch that he is become though young, a perfect master both for composition and performance on the organ and the harpsichord'. For others Chandos obtained positions in the Church, the Army and public service. The two Directors of Music mentioned above, Handel and Pepusch, were both financed and supported in their endeavours when they left Canons and went to London to promote opera and orchestral concerts. The sons of servants too were helped with their education, and we find Cassandra writing to her stepson, Lord Caernarvon, at Oxford, clearly with the intention of prompting him into a Chandos-like gesture:

> My Lord upon discussing with Dr. Friend concerning Cockran's son, and finding he thinks him fit for the University is willing to enter him a Commoner at Balliol College provided you think you have interest enough among the Fellows to get him chosen among the Schoolers next election and so to get him upon the foundation: and are willing to allow him £40 a year till that time, in consideration of his father's having been so long a servant of yours.

That Chandos's charitable gestures were instinctive and not merely used for effect is born out by his ready acceptance of responsibilities and reluctance to refuse help even in his later years as his means became less plentiful. When he felt unable to help, he preferred to give a refusal

George Frederick Handel

rather than raise false hopes, and although he undoubtedly enjoyed his importance, he did not over-estimate it nor welcome misplaced flattery and attention. 'My Lord says it would be a ridiculous thing for him to suffer himself to be prayed for in church by one who is not his chaplain,' wrote Cassandra to her sister-in-law Elizabeth Jacob who was hoping to induce Chandos to promise the chaplaincy in his household to one who was prepared to pray for him. And to many who presented him with samples of their work in order to procure his patronage, his secretary replied in terms similar to those addressed to Mr. Shelvocke in 1729:

> My Lord Duke commands me to acquaint you, that though it is very unusual with him to take Books upon the recommendation of their Authors, much less to accept of such sort of presents, yet His Grace is unwilling to put upon you the mortification of sending your Book back to you again, and has ordered me to pay you three Guineas as a Present for it. The Bearer hereof will deliver you the money and I must desire the favour of you to sign the Receipt which he will present to you.

In their letters, the Brydges of Tyberton and the Leighs of Adlestrop mentioned being at Canons in the company of other relatives, and choosing the right moment to approach the Duke with their requests for his interest or help; and had Chandos objected, presumably he would not have extended unlimited hospitality to potential supplicants. Similarly, outside the family, by becoming a Governor of the Charterhouse and of the Foundling Hospital, he laid himself open to further appeals; and his believing 'the instruction of poor children to be a very great charity' led him to maintain a number of schools in Herefordshire and one at Edgware.

Of course, Chandos's generosity could and did do little to halt the spread of serious deprivation that was beginning to affect the poorer classes and unskilled workers at the time. Real hardship was less obtrusive in the country than in the towns, because the population was sparser there, and still a majority of workers was able to find a livelihood in agriculture and domestic service. Nevertheless existing sources of charity – almshouses, bequests of food and clothing, schools such as Chandos helped to maintain – were increasingly necessary, and during his journeys through Gloucestershire, Worcestershire and Herefordshire, and visits to country houses in these areas, even if not from personal observation, then at any rate from conversations with local Justices of the Peace, Chandos must have been made aware of the problems of administering relief through the Poor Law and discouraging vagrancy and begging. For 'improving' landlords had already begun to make enclosures and to economise on labour, and industrial developments in the Midlands were exerting an influence that was to gain strength as the century went on, inducing both the hopeless and the enterprising to move to the new towns in the belief that life and work there offered better prospects than subsistence farming in rural areas had ever done.

In London though, the prevalence of poverty was undeniable and evidence of it quite inescapable. There always had been a shifting population without regular means of livelihood, and this was enormously increased during the 18th century as the capital exercised its irresistible attraction not only on the worthy in search of profitable employment but also on the less reputable, hopeful of engaging in criminal practices and remaining undetected among the teeming crowds and labyrinthine alleys to be found on the eastern side of the metropolis. By the 1720's and 1730's, the socially and politically eminent people were moving steadily westwards to live, leaving the Soho Square, Leicester Fields and Covent Garden areas to the bourgeoisie whose wealth was largely derived from overseas trade and banking; while further east and especially along by the river, shopkeepers, warehousemen, boatmen and all who contributed to the life and prosperity of the port of London, shared quarters and daily rubbed shoulders with the social misfits whose only means of subsistence were their own wits or the inability of others to protect themselves against crime. But there was no sharp dividing line between the rich and poor in London. Behind the houses of the wealthy and beyond the confines of the newly developed squares, there were uncleared slums that had once marked the limits of urban development, and were still inhabited by those who made a precarious living out of casual work for the rich – holding horses, carrying packages or messages, clearing rubbish, etc. – or out of effortless, spontaneous crime.

Thus it was impossible for anyone to walk or ride through the streets of London without seeing some poor dwellings, being importuned by beggars, or even set upon by thieves. That this state of affairs was so seldom remarked on in private letters and journals would seem to indicate that it was taken for granted. However, one of Chandos's cousins made a comment in a letter dated 1730, which reads not unlike a report of modern street violence:

> As for News, we are but very barren at present. I have been at ye Coffee-house on purpose to learn some news but hear little: all our

talk is about the Impudent Letter-senders. Several are taken up here and two have been tryed and aquitted. Certainly ye malice of ye world is such and ye Common peoples principles so bad, and with all the difficulty of getting a livelyhood so much greater than it has been, that I believe were it not for ye Law, they would robb, burn houses, Murder; nay Notwithstanding ye Law, it is done dayly here by some, 13 out of 17 are ordered for execution on Wednesday next, being thought a great many, and all for robbing in the Streets and Highways.[9]

Here is a sharp reminder that for those unfortunates, unable or unwilling – for whatever reason – to support themselves, and without the backing of a family or a well-intentioned employer, there was little public sympathy and rarely a second chance if they transgressed in any way.

CHAPTER 6

New Interests And Diversions

The Clerkships of the Hanaper & Sixpenny Writs obtained by Chandos during the early years of George I's reign, were virtually sinecures in that the small amount of work connected with them could easily be delegated to subordinates or the office farmed out to others. Similarly, his duties as Lord-Lieutenant of Herefordshire and Radnorshire were actually carried out by Deputies, and only serious local unrest or a national emergency of some kind would have obliged Chandos to appear in person to exercise his authority. This did not necessarily indicate negligence or inefficiency on his part, since from the inauguration of the office in the late 16th century, it had been recognised that the Lord Lieutenant might well be occupied elsewhere on state or personal business and therefore need subordinates to deputise for him locally. One matter referred to him concerned the loss of several important letters in the post, and 'the Mail being broken open ... and the letters thrown about the Stables of a common Inn'. Another source of trouble was connected with local opposition to the setting up of turnpikes which ranged from passive resistance to the payment of tolls, to the breaking down of gates and intimidation of the men in charge of them. In 1735, Chandos thought the news sufficiently disturbing to refer it to Lord Newcastle, the Secretary of State:

> The letter I have the honour to enclose to your Grace comes from ye Clerk of the Peace from Herefordshire and gives an account of a very extraordinary Tumult that has been by the abetment of the Turnpike cutters, flared up at Ross Fair. I thought it my Duty to lay it before your Grace.

Nine years later, during the Austrian Succession War and the scare of a possible French invasion, Chandos had to send word to his Deputies 'to seize all arms belonging to Papists and others judged dangerous to the peace of the kingdom and to put the laws against these people into execution' – laws which, incidentally, Chandos himself had helped to pass while a member of the House of Commons, and which at the time (1700) he had described as 'very hard, but ye only effectual means to extirpate Popery out of this kingdom . . . so high are ye Roman Catholics grown in all parts'.

Active work connected with the Rangership of Enfield Chace was also left to subordinates, but Chandos was responsible for the state of the property (leased from the Duchy of Lancaster) and he found himself involved in endless worries about the renting out of the lodges which were in an advanced state of dilapidation, and almost continuous hostilities with poachers, illicit wood-cutters and deer-slayers. What he had taken on as a sure source of profit and (he imagined) a sinecure, proved completely otherwise, though it was not without its uses, when he could write as follows to his Deputy Ranger:

> The occasion of my giving you this present trouble is to desire you'll order a Buck (if there are any yet in Season) to be killed this evening and sent over to Cannons early tomorrow morning. I have a good deal of Company to dine with me and should be glad to treat them with a piece of Venison.[1]

In comparison, the Stewardship of the town of St. Andrews, while conferring a certain status, must have seemed much less burdensome. This was offered to Chandos in 1721, probably as a kind of quid pro quo, because it followed a visit there by his sons during which they had been generously entertained, and in return for which hospitality Chandos pressed gifts of money on the town to be used for charitable purposes, and sufficient means on the University to establish a Chair of Medicine and Anatomy.

It will be remembered that after resigning his Paymastership in 1713, Chandos had deliberately avoided taking on any time-consuming public office, so as to be free to devote himself to other interests. After 1719, in addition to his investments in trading companies, his attention became increasingly centred on his houses, property development and other new ventures. His concern to provide his own residence with a decent water supply led to a commitment to the York Water Company, a waterworks built on the site of Old York House in the Strand and supplying houses in the surrounding area. This proved only a limited success since the company was in competition with the New River Company which in the long run proved the more profitable of the two. A better proposition was Chandos's investment in the Sun Fire Insurance Company, a typical

York Buildings and Water Works

contemporary innovation and one of several companies founded to protect properties in the capital from a repetition of the Great Fire of 1666. Those who subscribed to such schemes received a badge to fix to their houses so that these could be indentified by the fire-fighters (usually Thames watermen) who arrived carrying leather buckets and hoses, and wheeling tanks of water, to deal with the conflagration. That the tanks and hoses were also advocated for watering gardens, and leather fire-buckets – suitably painted – for ornamental use in entrance halls, raises grave doubts as to the effectiveness of this equipment in the face of serious fires.

From time to time, Chandos initiated new projects himself. His eagerness to exploit the possibilities of Britain's expanding trade, and unfailing confidence in his own propensity for commercial developments, had led him in turn to attempt the promotion of oyster fisheries off the Essex coast, warehousing and wharfage on the Thames at Scotland Yard, and the opening up of areas for settlement and development in Norway, Nova Scotia and New York. So firm was his belief in the future of this last place, that he claimed had he been a younger man, he would have gone there to seek his fortune. Scientific leanings, as well as a desire for profit, prompted his interest in various exploratory mines – for coal, lead, copper and silver – in the Midlands, Cornwall, Somerset and on his own estates in Herefordshire and Radnorshire. Some of the ores extracted, he tested in his own laboratory at Canons, though he could only handle small quantities there. Some he handed over to others to deal with:

> I desire you'll be so good to get it (the crude ore) essayed by one of the best Refineries you can hear of, to see if it contains any Metall either of Silver, Copper or Lead. I think the charge of Essaying is half a guinea. I likewise send you two papers of different sorts of Mundick, one contains three ounces and the other two: the one is from Somerset, the other from Radnorshire. I should be glad if you could prevail with Mrs. Coppin to make a tryal of these to see what her art will produce from them and whether she can succeed better in these tryals than she did in the last.[2]

This trust in Mrs. Coppin who claimed to have a secret formula for extracting silver from certain rocks would seem to indicate that Chandos's outlook was not based exclusively on scientific reasoning. Despite endless experimental ventures, his luck – or his judgment? – remained uniformly bad. One man Cowell, who was engaged to smelt copper for him, was accused of being 'a most vile as well as an ungrateful fellow' and clearly held responsible for the misdeeds of the workers under his direction whom Chandos considered needed watching all the time, 'there being nothing more easy than for them to Steal small quantities of the Copper from time to time, by lading it into little pots, which to be sure they would not fail to bring with them on purpose concealed for such a Roguery. Cowell shall never be employed again by me.'[3]

The most promising of all Chandos's schemes initially seemed to be his plans for the development of Bridgewater in Somerset, since these involved building, industry and trade. The ultimate objective here was the creation of a port that would rival Bristol in the volume and variety of its trade and the prosperity of its citizens. To this end, Chandos bought the greater part of the existing town from its owner, had the old houses pulled down, and put into the hands of a local architect-carpenter, Benjamin Holloway, the planning and erection of new houses to accommodate the present population and the many more who were expected to flock to work in the new town. Industries – brick-making, glass-blowing, brewing and soap-manufacturing were planned to provide employment and produce goods for export via the newly-canalised River Parret and the Bristol Channel. However, the project scarcely got started. Basically it was unrealistic, and this fact coupled with Chandos's impatience and fatally bad choice of collaborators, made failure inevitable. Holloway's houses, intended to be 'substantial, not like London houses which are supposed not to stand above 20 or 30 years' were built without proper foundations and of poorly made bricks, and even though Edward Shepherd, Chandos's London architect, was sent down to Bridgewater to supervise work there, he produced no better results. The planned industries also failed to materialise because the right raw materials could not be assembled, and Richard Salter – Chandos's adviser in these matters – proved no more than 'a plausible imposter'.

Although Chandos steadily extended the range of his commitments as time went on, building remained one of his over-riding interests. Not content with his London dwellings and out-of-town house at Canons, he acquired yet more properties during the 1720's, with the idea of making use of some of them, even if only for short periods. One of these was the Mynd in Herefordshire. Taken over some years earlier from its owner, a Mr. Pye, who was in debt to him, Chandos had used the estate as a source of supplies for Canons – horses, cattle and deer being kept there, cider and beer brewed, grain and fruit grown and stored. During the 1720's, seemingly with the idea of its being turned into a country residence, improvements were made to the house, craftsmen who had worked at Canons being sent down to instal new fireplaces, ceilings and windows. The house has now disappeared so we have no means of judging how it compared with Chandos's London properties; certainly he can have made little use of it himself, since he decided to sell it within a few years.

A much more rewarding step was the purchase in 1726 of Shaw Hall near Reading. Although the property was in a dilapidated state, needing both modernisation and repair, and although the terms of the sale were devious (among other things they involved the buyer in paying for the education and the upbringing of the heir of the previous owner John Talbot) nevertheless Chandos pushed ahead with his plans, which in the end afforded him much satisfaction and happiness. The house had been a small Elizabethan manor, and primarily the features of its Tudor origin – mullioned windows, wainscotted rooms and a small formal garden – had to be removed and replaced by 18th century innovations – 'handsome large sashes of glass', plastered ceilings and wall, decorative fireplaces and a more elaborate and impressive layout of the grounds. Many defects and deficiences were revealed as work proceeded, and Edward Shepherd was sent from London to direct the efforts of local men – a carpenter, a cabinet maker, an ironmonger, a plumber and others. All the trouble proved worthwhile in the long run because Chandos and Duchess Cassandra used Shaw Hall regularly as a stopping place on their way to and from Bath, and as a haven of rest when the pressures of city life proved too much for them. Frequently, having gone there for a few days, they stayed for several weeks, and both were clearly enamoured of the place, as – in due course – was Chandos's third wife Lydia, who chose to spend her remaining years there, after her husband's death. Shaw was unpretentious, comfortable and welcoming rather than grand or elegant, and its grounds were planned to please rather then impress. Both Chandos and Cassandra approved of the fashion of having water-effects in a garden, so John Hore, their water engineer, introduced a fish pond, a cascade and a canal, the River Lambourne being conveniently near as a source of supply. Cassandra also loved trees and shady walks, so 'baubling pedestals and figures' were removed to make way for green lawns and yew hedges.

Chandos's other building venture was at Bath, where – he decided – he must have a house of his own, since he and his wife were finding their visits to the spa determined not by their own needs and inclinations, but according to whether and when lodgings were available. The standard of accommodation too seemed unsatisfactory, perhaps by comparison with

Shaw Hall, Newbury

the comfort they were used to elsewhere, although Cassandra from her visits as a young woman to the spas at Harrogate and Scarborough must have been aware of the atrocious food, dirty lodgings and general lack of amenities that had to be endured by those seeking relief from symptoms of ill-health.

The property that Chandos bought was in the vicinity of the Cross Bath, adjoining St. John's Hospital, at this time a hospice for poor people. Here there was a court, with the hospital and lodging houses occupying three sides, while the fourth overlooked the city wall near the West Gate, beyond which lay open land as yet unbuilt on. Chandos considered the lodgings 'objectionable to a person of fashion because they did not afford a dressing room and dining room beside the room he lyes in, especially if he had his lady with him', so he despatched his architect John Wood (the elder) from London to plan alterations that would make the accommodation more spacious and more private; and with the help of the Duchess equipped the rooms more adequately with curtains, hangings and screens from Canons and with furniture bought locally in Bath. Potential users of the lodgings were promised fresh air, gardens to walk in, and an uninterrupted prospect of the hills surrounding the city; but like most of Chandos's undertakings, this was rushed into without the access rights of the residents of the Hospital being assured or the respective positions of the new owner and the resident tenants (who looked after the lodgings) being clearly defined. Consequently, it was only after numerous and acrimonious arguments with the landladies, local workmen and neighbouring property owners that the Duke acquired the accommodation he wanted, although to his satisfaction it was soon acknowledged as 'the best and most envied in Bath'.

So the Duke and Duchess now had residences in London and at Edgware: a retreat for relaxation or a stopping place on the way to the west at Shaw Hall: and their own quarters to stay in when they were at Bath. They enjoyed going here and to Tunbridge Wells, to mitigate the effects of their hectic social life in London, and in Cassandra's case, to seek relief from the headaches and fainting fits that plagued her all her life. The cold waters of Tunbridge suited her better than the brackish springs at Bath, but both were more tolerable than the cures she had tried at the northern spas when she was younger. In spite of being mooted as a rest cure (visitors to Tunbridge Wells were even forbidden to put pen to paper) life at a fashionable spa in the early 18th century was anything but this, for it was ruled by conventions that were as rigidly applied as any that obtained in London society, so that visitors found it

The Bath House, Tunbridge Wells

The Pantiles, Tunbridge Wells

New Interests and Diversions

difficult to withdraw from the daily round and please themselves to any extent.

At the fashionable spas the mornings were spent drinking or bathing in the waters, then according to Macky,

> the Company returns, some to go to Church and some to the Coffee Houses where one is very well informed of what passes in the world. After Prayers all the Company appear on the walks in the greatest Splendour, Musick playing all the time; and the Ladies and Gentlemen divert themselves with Raffling, Hazard, drinking of tea and walking till two, when they go to Dinner.

Both Tunbridge Wells and Bath had many shops, some to supply necessities like groceries and meat, but many more to tempt those who had very little to fill their time except to indulge their fancy for new clothes, jewellery or trinkets. As Macky reported: 'The Manner of living at Tunbridge Wells is very diverting for one week; but as there is no variety but in new faces, it soon becomes tiresome to a Stranger'. Boredom also gave rise to the scandalous rumours which provided the main topic of conversation and occasionally spurred the young and the not so young to indiscreet affairs. However, as time went on and the spas were taken over by the fashionable world during the season, social life became much as it was in London. 'Company and diversion is in short the main business of these places'.(Defoe) As early as 1703, even before Bath had reached the height of its popularity as a resort, Mary Leigh wrote to her husband:

> There's an abundance of Company here, more than has been known so early in the year for several years. The Queen intending to come to the Bath in August makes people flock down that came for health before. There's plays 3 times a week and Musick in the Grove the other nights; but no Balls yet.[4]

By the 1720's entertainments had become even more numerous and more elaborate; expeditions by day into the surrounding countryside to view the landscape and visit places of interest: al fresco picnics and dancing by night had become regular features of the social round. Personal expense accounts which included subscriptions to lending libraries, 'the Musick', money lost at cards, payments to various shopkeepers and hair dressers, are an indication of other ways in which time was spent.

Journeys across country, whether to resorts such as the spas, or to make private visits, were not to be undertaken lightly. Although a few of the main roads in the vicinity of London had been turnpiked by the early years of the 18th century, travel mostly involved the use of unmade tracks, with no direction posts and few respectable or reliable stopping places for changing horses or for refreshment, except in the towns. Planning a journey from Bath to Barnsley in 1731, Chandos hoped to manage the 26 miles in one day to avoid an overnight stop, but realised that since his servants did not know the way, he might well be held up. A few years later, in 1735, Lord Lichfield travelling the same route from Bath to Ditchley via Cirencester, reported:

> Hither (Cirencester) safe after a very bad journey, the ways being excessive bad, and tho' we had two setts of Horses, found itt a very difficult matter to reach this place . . . and to mend all, wee lost our way about five miles off in a very wett night which hindered us above an hour, and one of my Horses hung his hind leg in a Deep Rut so that we were forced to dig him out.

Chandos kept a large stable of horses, Arabians for riding, Hanoverian greys for drawing his coaches, and English breeds for heavier work. Both he and Duchess Cassandra were fond of riding, but their longer journeys were made by post chaise or coach, necessary household supplies being sent ahead by wagon to wherever they were going. For people like them with estates to provide their basic needs, staying away from home was not as expensive as for those who had to buy food and domestic necessities on the spot. (Prices in Tunbridge Wells and Bath were notoriously high, largely because so many farmers and their families came in from the surrounding countryside with the specific intention of making what profits they could during the fashionable season). As far as we know, Chandos and his wife met with few adventures while travelling; their horses bolted on one occasion while they were riding on Bushey Heath and their coach overturned one dark night as they were returning from Bath. But the times and circumstances could be dangerous for road-users. In 1719, as reported in the *Original Weekly Journal*, one of the workmen going home from Edgware with his week's pay was 'robb'd, stript naked and left bound in a ditch 24 hours, near Highgate' and Chandos himself was set upon by two highwaymen in the next year. There was no guarantee of safety even in the heart of London. After 1714 Fortnum and Mason supplied an armed escort with all orders over £5 delivered outside the St. James's area.

With Shaw Hall kept in a state of readiness for use, and relatives living in Oxfordshire and Gloucestershire, the Duke and Duchess had little

The Road to Bath

need of inns and posting-houses. At Oxford, Chandos's nephew, Dr. Theophilus Leigh, was Master of Balliol College, and here and at Adlestrop the well-known family hospitality prevailed. The Leigh's house had not yet been subjected to improvement (as it was to be later by Sanderson Miller) so it was much as it had been during the previous century when William Leigh had turned a large barn into a comfortable family home and laid out the grounds with an orangery, a lake and a plot for the flowers which his wife Joanna loved so much. Adlestrop was situated on the main road between Oxford and Gloucester via Chipping Norton, not yet turnpiked but much used by coach travellers and riders, and carriers with goods destined for local markets. The Leighs were an exceptionally affectionate family, always ready to receive relatives and friends from further afield, and during their visits to draw them into an established circle of local connections and acquaintances. The Chamberlaynes at Maugersbury, the Walters at Sarsden, the Hastings at Daylesford and the Jones at Chastleton all lived within easy reach in manor houses that had belonged to their families since the Reformation, survived the impact of the Civil Wars and were now being brought up to date in a modest way, with improved architectural features, more attractive grounds and indications of the cultural tastes of their owners in the shape of pictures, libraries and musical instruments. Members of these families recommended domestic servants, nursemaids, midwives and craftsmen to each other, lent books, exchanged plants and seeds, compared notes about their estates and carried out commissions when they went on journeys. Their letters reveal an intimate knowledge of the health and activities of other members of their circle and a genuine concern for their well-being.

If Chandos was intending to visit his estates in Radnorshire and Herefordshire or relatives in Shropshire, he would go on from Adlestrop to Troy in Monmouthshire, used as a residence by the Dukes of Beaufort after the destruction of Raglan Castle during the Civil Wars. Although by no means as magnificent a building as Badminton and without such extensive grounds, Troy was nevertheless a substantial mansion, comfortable within and impressive outside with extensive gardens and a deer park. Also on the road to Hereford was Kentchurch, home of the Scudamore family, related to the Brydges by marriage and much in demand as god-parents. Their house had mediaeval origins, but each generation had incorporated improvements to the building and grounds so that like Troy it had an imposing appearnace that reflected the social status of its owners.

New Interests and Diversions 115

When Bath was their destination, the Duke and Duchess frequently stopped at Barnsley, first with Brereton Bourchier and his wife in what is now Barnsley House, and then in the dwelling newly built by Henry Perrot during the early 1720's. Barnsley was situated not far from the main road to Cirencester, and Perrot's house offered a peaceful atmosphere and elegant surroundings to those who stayed there. Chandos and his wife must have noticed many similarities between the architecture and decorations of Barnsley Park and those of other friends involved in new building projects. As well as an interest in politics and business, Chandos shared with Perrot a concern for estate management and improvement, an obsessive interest in remedies for various ailments, and an almost boyish enthusiasm for scientific instruments. Perrot owned a telescope, much admired (and envied?) by the Duke who took delight in trying it out and then ordering one that he hoped would be better still.

> It (Perrot's) is undoubtedly an exceeding good one . . . but I must own it does not take in so large a compass as that I had before . . . because mine is very near as long again as yours, wch is but 11 Inches. I think to write to Mr. Short at Edinburgh to desire him to make me one three foot long, and if he can make one of that length proportionately as good as this, it will be an extraordinary Telescope.[5]

Among the visitors to Chandos's London homes was Lord Bathurst who was improving his house and grounds at Cirencester during the 1720's. It is not known whether Chandos ever visited him there, although Cirencester Park is close to Barnsley and on the road to Bath, but inevitably he must have taken an interest in Bathurst's plans and aspirations since these were commonly discussed and criticised among the members of their circle jointly concerned with contemporary London developements – Lords Burlington, Harcourt and Bingley for instance. Having acquired an extensive area to add to his estate from Chandos's niece Arabella Atkyns (and at a bargain price according the Chandos) Bathurst sought the advice of his friends including Alexander Pope, as to how to lay out the grounds in an interesting and impressive manner; and no doubt Pope's dictum, 'Planting is as critical as building in the creation of an estate' helped to explain the subsequent scale of his tree-planting and the bold pattern of the avenues radiating from the house to reach the furthermost parts of the park, which were comparable with the Duke of Beaufort's layout of his grounds at Badminton.

One place that was usually the specific object of the journey because not on the road to anywhere, was Wanstead House. Duchess Cassandra had known it as a home, though not a very happy one, during the first few years of her mother's second marriage to Sir Josiah Child, and had lost no time in escaping from it when the opportunity offered. However, even before her step-father's death in 1699, she had been back to visit her mother, and after that date was there quite often as she was fond of and interested in her half-brother Sir Richard Child and his family. After their marriage, family ties and the interest Chandos shared with Sir Richard in politics, investments and building, often took the Duke and Duchess to Wanstead. Although the new house was not on the scale originally proposed by Colen Campbell (which would have made it larger than Blenheim) it was neverthless significant, and surrounded by grounds intended to make it an English Versailles, and Child's hospitality ran on regal lines to match. Like Chandos, he frequently entertained 'Foriegn Ministers and other Persons of Distiction', but the arrangements at Wanstead seem to have been less regimented than at Canons, and the guests, instead of ending the evening listening to a dignified recital of music, might well be entertained with 'a neat Cold Collation and Diversion at Quadrille till Twelve at Night and then dancing till about Five'.

As with their circumstances, Chandos and his wife were for the most part fortunate in their families and their friends. Earlier in life, when she had made long journeys with her brother, Cassandra had most often sought hospitality and shelter with relatives or tenants of the family, and only when travelling in remote parts of Yorkshire or when staying at the spas, had she been thrown back on wayside inns or hired lodging houses. Now, as a married couple, the Duke and Duchess had ports of call throughout the southern counties and the west country where they were sure of a welcome whether their coming had been announced or not. Seemingly, within their circle, letters informed when people were on the move, and those who were at home held themselves in readiness to receive visitors. In 1698, the Marchioness of Worcester wrote to Mrs. Leigh at Adlestrop to inform her:

> I had a very well come letter from Mrs. Jacob by the last post with an account of the happy matches that are going foreward in your family. If you plees to acquaint my sister Willoughby as I have by this post done in a letter to my mother, of our desire of comeing to you which I hope will be according to my wishes to the satisfaction of you. . . . I believe Sir Thomas Willoughby cannot be with you so

Wanstead House

> soon as you think; by what we understand of theire journey when they were hear, they could not.

Sometimes they were disappointed because adverse weather conditions or an overlong stay in one place caused travellers to change their route; sometimes unheralded arrivals were followed by extended visits, but all these variations on the theme were taken calmly, and more often than not, once a nucleus of visitors had assembled, others were invited, especially if the company favoured a game of cards as was frequently the case. Thus, in October 1729, the Duke sent a hasty summons to Mr. Capper, an attorney friend:

> I give you the trouble of this only to put you in mind of the hopes you gave me of your and Sir Francis' company here on Friday at Dinner and as Colonel Inwood is obliged to be at the Tower on Guard all the latter part of this week, I should be glad if you'd bring a third along with you to make a party at Whist.

Visitors might be asked to convey messages, accompany children, or deliver goods en route, and these services helped to draw the family together and cement the bonds of friendship. For foreign news or the latest political developments, those who lived outside London might have to wait for the delivery of news-letters, but for the announcements of births, marriages and deaths, news of the progress of invalids, business undertakings and investments, the ground had usually been well prepared beforehand. The unexpected was always reported and received with an element of surprise, so stable was the world of the Brydges, the Leighs, the Childs and their like. Chandos wrote to Henry Perrot in December 1731:

> Being persuaded that you'll take no small pleasure in hearing any piece of good fortune that befalls our family, I can't forbear acquainting you that we were playing a party of Quadrille this afternoon, and about nine, Lady Caernarvon said she found herself uneasy and desired to go up and about a quarter of an hour ago was safely brought to bed of a fine boy.

This was the grandchild that Chandos had long been hoping for, since his elder son's offspring were both daughters, and Henry's first child had been a girl too. No wonder the event called for the immediate despatch of letters to members of the family.

CHAPTER 7

Chandos And His Fellow Builders.

Leaving aside the eulogies of Charles Gildon (*The Vision:* 1718) and Samuel Humphreys (*Canons:* 1728) whose descriptions of Canons were as exaggeratedly baroque as any painting or ornament that graced the subject of their verses, we still have the writings of more sober observers – John Macky and Daniel Defoe for instance – to impress on us its outstanding grandeur and magnificence. Both these were judging Canons in comparison with other stately homes they had seen in the course of their travels round the country, so that its features must have been outstanding even if not quite as spectacular as they maintained. 'Inferior to few Royal Palaces in Europe' stated Macky; and 'so Beautiful so Lofty and so Majestic that a Pen can ill describe it' wrote Defoe. In size certainly it was not as immense as Blenheim, nor were its grounds as elaborately contrived as those at Boughton or Wilton; all the same it was distinctive enough in appearance and sufficiently decorative in its furnishings to hold its own with, and even surpass in some respects other contemporary creations, which was of course what Chandos had hoped for.

The first three decades of the 18th century were years of great commercial expansion and – despite the Spanish War which ended in 1713 – of comparative peace and prosperity for the people of England. As the Whigs had foreseen, the economic gains from the war helped very considerably to offset its costs to the country, and in due course, not just the trading vessels that now had many more ports of call to use, but the investors in the companies that owned the ships, those who supplied the cargoes to fill them, and those who used or sold the products they brought back, were all enriched. A Whig government led by Sir Robert Walpole who believed in taxing as little as possible and avoiding all controversial issues, ensured that much of the increasing national wealth remained in people's pockets and was available to be spent on whatever might afford pleasure or satisfaction. For many this meant the pursuit of a more comfortable standard of living; in the case of Chandos and his friends the achievement of what was best in the way of architecture, amenities and decoration in their homes, and most beautiful (according to contemporary ideas) in the lay-out of their surroundings – the jewel and the setting were to be worthy of each other, in fact.

That the ambitions and activities of men such as Chandos should have led to developments in the spheres of all the arts, was also a result of contemporary political and social circumstances. In 1714 Queen Anne – least fitted of all the Stuart rulers to give a cultural lead to the country – was succeeded by George I, a stranger to England and its people; and he was followed in 1727 by George II, more interested, except for music, in the arts of war than of peace; thus patronage and trend-setting passed from the Court to members of the aristocracy who had the means and inclination to undertake this responsibility. Most of them had travelled abroad to complete their education, had seen for themselves the wave of new building that was taking place in France and Germany, and studied the inspiration of this in the Renaissance palaces and villas of Italy. While abroad, they bought books on architecture, drawings and plans, and became acquainted with the work of decorative painters, sculptors, stuccoists and other craftsmen, some of whom were encouraged by the enthusiasm of the English travellers to come to England in due course, in search of commissions. Artistic tastes were therefore being formed by observation, experience and study, and it was not surprising that when books such as Leoni's translation of Palladio's views on architecture and Colen Campbell's *Vitruvius Britannicus* appeared, they quickly became respected works of reference, and those who followed the precepts therein, entitled to be regarded as arbiters of what was right and desirable architecturally speaking. Other contemporary publications included folios of engravings of houses and gardens, and the popularity of these indicate a widespread interest and appeal. In time it was not just Lord Bathurst or Lord Bingley who were visiting their friends' houses but the public generally, for whom guides to the respective 'seats' and catalogues of pictures and sculptures were produced. Thus what at first was appreciated by a few congnoscenti came in time to be accepted as a recommendation, by many.

Another feature of the times, helpful both to potential patrons and those whom they employed, was the emergence of professional architects who began to take over the role of the master-masons. The latter, until the mid-17th century, had been responsible for all stages in the design and construction of houses. Their work was never original and never grandiose, and although not all such builders were as unscrupulous or notorious as Nicholas Barbon – 'who found it not worth his while to deal little: his intent was only in great undertaking' – nevertheless their overriding aim was to make money out of successful contracting, so that they had little inclination to experiment or to indulge in expensive materials or methods. During the late 17th century however, thanks to various important public commissions undertaken by Christopher Wren, Nicholas Hawksmoor, Sir John Vanbrugh and James Gibbs, there appeared a number of architects who were not themselves actively involved in building although they might assume complete responsibility for the engagement and supervision of workmen, choice and purchase of materials and ultimate outcome of the venture. Only some of them had had a professional training – Vanbrugh, for instance, had been a soldier, a playwright and Clarenceux King of Arms before turning to architecture – but all had original ideas, the courage of their convictions and a capacity for pushing their plans through to completion.

A position in the Royal Works was an achievement in itself and much coveted by the professionally ambitious for whom there was as yet little scope in independent practice. As the superiority of 'architects' houses became established however, the demand for professional services increased, and once their ability had been proved, with or without the backing of the Royal Works, commissions began to come their way. It is interesting to note that at the same time, a special relationship sprang up between the architect and his patron, based on mutual respect, shared tastes and in some cases shared knowledge and experience. Vanbrugh, Thomas Archer and Gibbs were as well educated and widely travelled as their employers and accepted by them socially, while Chandos, Burlington, Bingley and other members of their circle had looked critically at a large number of buildings and owned folios and drawings of architectural designs as well as expensive sets of mathematical instruments, which Burlington and Bingley at any rate, knew how to use. There were also shared ambitions, in so far as the architects recognised and subscribed to the new ventures as an indication of the success already achieved by their promoters in public life, and as a promise of success to come for themselves. It was in fact to the advantage of both parties that the outcome of the work undertaken should provoke interest, admiration and even envy.

Where patrons and architects moved in the same circles, one successful commission almost inevitably led to others within the group, so it is not surprising that we can follow the progress of reputable architects from one great house to another. Quite a number of these experts at some time were employed by Chandos in his various building projects. His first appointment at Canons was of William Talman, grown old by now (1713) and temperamentally even more difficult than he had been when working for William Blathwayt at Dyrham (Gloucestershire) or the Duke of Devonshire at Chatsworth. On the grounds that his charges were exorbitant: 'I cannot believe anyone who has the character of a gentleman can make so ridiculous and extravagant a demand', Chandos dismissed Talman and took on John James, an Office of Works employee, already known for this work on St. Paul's and other city churches, and his translation of an Italian treatise on perspective. However, the duke seems to have had reservations about James's competence since he asked Vanbrugh to oversee the work that was in progress. In a letter of instruction to James, he wrote: 'There are several alterations which I think will be necessary to be made in the part of Cannons you have been concerned in, which I must entreat favour of you to call upon Sir John Vanbrugh about, who will explain them better to you upon the plans than I can by letter.' Vanbrugh had himself been Comptroller of the Royal Works after satisfactorily completing Castle Howard for his patron Lord Carlisle, and as well as designing London houses, now had the glory of Blenheim to his credit; so through both recommendations and achievement he had become known and was popular. His services at Canons, probably confined to comments on designs, were not required for long because Chandos parted with James quite soon, dissatisfied with his efforts.

James's place was taken in 1715 by James Gibbs, whose ideas and work were in every respect typical of the new professional architect. Wealthy, well-educated, widely travelled, a Fellow of the Royal Society, he moved freely among his patrons and was accepted as their social equal. He regarded craftsmen-builders as 'common workmen' and believed firmly that an architect must be a true professional, able to decide every detail of the work in hand, and then to make everything contribute to his overall conception of the finished product. Gibbs established his reputation by outstanding work on city churches, most notably St. Martin in the Fields, and after being at Canons was to go on to the Cavendish Square development and its church of St. Peter's, to public buildings in Oxford and Cambridge, and to Ditchley Park where he worked for Lord Lichfield, a friend of the Leighs at Adlestrop, Lord Bathurst at Cirencester, and the Duke of Shrewsbury who lived at Heythrop House nearby.

Ralph Allen's House, Bath

Prior Park, Bath

John Price, Chandos's next appointment at Canons (in 1720) was not of the same calibre as Gibbs, although like the latter he had worked on London churches previously, and later went on to design the new house for Chandos in Cavendish Square (never actually built) which was intended to be as magnificent as Canons itself. His drawings of the two houses show the resemblances in style and are indeed our clearest guide as to Chandos's plans for them. Edward Shepherd followed Price in 1722 and was recommended to Chandos by Lord Bingley who had been invited to Canons in 1719 to give his opinion of the work in hand.

> By the time your Lordship returns, I hope my little building will be advanc'd so far as for one to be able to make a guess what appearance it will have; and it shou'd be such an one as is displeasing to your Lordship, I shall pull it down with more satisfaction then I carry it up . . .

Shepherd was an innovator (much under the Palladian influence of Colen Campbell) who after working at Canons, designed two smaller houses for Chandos in Cavendish Square in place of the larger on planned by Price; he was then sent on to Shaw Hall to supervise the innovations there, and lastly went to Bath where, in a sense, he prepared the way for John Wood, in so far as his plans for Chandos's building projects there were handed on to Wood to carry out. Wood, like Shepherd, was a protégé of Lord Bingley and first employed by him in Yorkshire. He then came to London, and worked with Shepherd in connection with the Grosvenor and Cavendish Square developments, before being summoned to Bath by Chandos. In due course he was taken under the wing of Ralph Allen to help him exploit the potentialities of the building stone in his quarries, and to build him an elegant town house and a mansion at prior Park closely resembling Campbell's Wanstead in sophistication and elegance. Ultimately, Wood branched out on his own, planning the layout and beginning the construction in the centre of Bath of the great squares and crescents (completed by his son John Wood II) that were to transform what had been an old market town into the leading spa and social centre of England.

Of the other architects employed within the same circle of patrons though not by Chandos himself, there was Thomas Archer, essentially a gentleman architect, who like Gibbs trained in Rome and brought back influences that were reflected in his work for the Duke of Devonshire at Chatsworth and for the Duke of Shrewsbury at Heythrop, the latter being one of the most Italianate houses ever to be built in England. Colen

Campbell, author of *Vitruvius Britannious*, ultimately a source of blueprints for many other architects and local draftsmen, was employed by Sir Richard Child to plan the new house he built on the site of his father's manor at Wanstead: and in this establishment he reached a peak of excellence that many a noble builder sought to emulate. The example of Wanstead persuaded Lord Burlington to employ Campbell to help in the remodelling of Burlington House in London and supply a design for his out-of-town house at Chiswick. Burlington was also the patron of William Kent who during the course of his career turned his hand to painting, architecture and landscape design and in turn served Burlington, Lord Lichfield at Ditchley and Sir Charles Cottrell at Rousham, a near neighbour. Also combining the roles of both patron and architect were Lord Bingley, an acknowledged connoisseur and one of the earliest English advocates of European culture: Lord Bathurst who after retiring from politics devoted all his time, attention and money to the improvement of his house and estate at Cirencester: and Lord Burlington who had returned from a Grand Tour of Italy at the age of twenty with a consuming passion for architecture which never left him. As a practising designer, a collector and publisher of important works on architecture, and a discerning patron of promising talent, he was outstanding. Perhaps the measure of his influence lies in the fact that he reconciled insular English taste to essentially Palladian (i.e. Italian) buildings, such as his own villa at Chiswick, which so caught the imagination of the local inhabitants that one of the advertised attractions at the Royal Swan Inn, along with King Arthur's knife and fork and Adam's key to the front and back doors of the Garden of Eden, was 'a model of Lord Burlington's house, made in Baccopipe clay in 4 days, curiously done'.[1]

As has been mentioned the relationship between architects and patrons underwent a change during the early years of the 18th century. Whatever the form of the contract drawn up in the respect of a particular commission, the employer almost always was prepared to leave the conduct of the work in the hands of the designer. There might be, and in fact usually was, consultation about materials and the details of decoration but this mostly took the form of recommendation and acquiescence rather than an argument from entrenched positions. We have already noticed Chandos's tendency to impatience, and fair but not over-generous remuneration of his architects. Except perhaps with Shepherd (was the latter a less forceful character than some of the others?) he does not seem to have been on as familiar and easy terms with his architects as he was with some of his employees, or as were other patrons. In fact he was rather out of date in his unwillingness to respect and allow the degree of responsibility they were prepared and able to take. His fury over Talman's charges for the journeys made between Canons and London is, for instance, in direct contrast with the claims that William Blathwayt's architect Hauderoy was allowed to make and the special favours shown him by the servants during his visits to Dyrham:

> Pd for 7 pullitts spent when Mr Hauderoy was at Dyrham:
> Pd to Mary Penney and Mary Jordan for Pies, fruite, Sugar etc spent upon Mr Hauderoy.
> Pd for a Quire of Paper for Mr. Hauderoy.

Lord Lichfield seems to have accepted criticism of the state of his house from Francis Smith, without demur:

> My Lord, your back Stair Cases are very small and very dark. . . . The Bedchambers are very little rooms notwithstanding the Addition of the Bow windows which circular break I cannot think will be any handsom ornaments in the front of such a building. . . .[2]

And at all the houses that have been mentioned, local craftsmen worked amicably and successfully under the direction of the architect, with very little if any interference from the owner of the property. (The Duchess of Marlborough's dealing with Vanbrugh were, of course, a notable exception). If final proof were needed that architects had now arrived socially as well as professionally, we can find it in their building or purchasing for themselves houses not very different from those they were designing for their patrons. Kent had his own rooms in Burlington House, but Gibbs and Price lived round the corner from Cavendish Square, Vanbrugh had a house at Greenwich, and Archer ultimately retired to a country mansion and the leisured life of a country gentleman.

As a result of their regular employment at one great house after another, some of the fashionable architects built up an association with key workers who moved about with them from one job to another. These men were capable of interpreting the architects' designs and skilled in working in their own medium – stone, wood, marble, iron etc., and in turn they decided whether further subsidiary help was needed and how it should be deployed. Vanbrugh, for instance, used William Townsend of Oxford and Edward Strong, one of the quarrying family of Taynton, in his projects at Oxford and Blenheim. Thomas Archer favoured Francis Smith of Warwick who worked with him at Heythrop, and Smith was also used by James Gibbs at nearby Ditchley. At Shaw Hall, Jonathan

Dyrham Park

Hicks, a carpenter-mason was instructed by Chandos to carry out Shepherd's designs for improving the house and buildings in the grounds. At Bridgwater under Shepherd's supervision Benjamin Holloway directed the actual building. The publication of books of designs by professional architects, many with details of window-frames, doorways and other ornamental features, was making it possible for an increasing number of workmen to have access to these and explains why it is not always easy to determine whether an architect directed certain work personally or whether his ideas were interpreted and executed by an ingenious and astute local worker. One house which has so far defied all the attempts of the experts to determine its architect and the craftsmen who worked on it is Barnsley Park, built between 1719-31 by Chandos's nephew by marriage Henry Perrot. Nicholas Hawksmoor, John Price and John James have all been suggested as possible designers, and the excellence of many of its decorative features has been taken as proof that more sophisticated skills than those of local workmen were involved in the achievement of these. 'It is a sumptuous edifice in the high Italian style, where, in a very magnificent saloon, are fresco paintings by the best masters' commented Rudder. No written records remain in connection with the building of the house, but the fact that this took place at much the same time as Canons was being completed and work at Ditchley was going on, makes it seem possible that some of the same craftsmen were employed at all three. We do know that Chandos corresponded regularly with Perrot, was interested in his activities, visited Barnsley and admired the house.

Locally, whether in London or in the country, the building projects of wealthy landowners were a most useful source of employment, and the account books and bills of many families show that the same carpenters, joiners, stonemasons, slaters, smiths, bricklayers etc. were used whenever major operations, alterations or repairs needed to be done. Sometimes a particular skill was handed down in a family, and sons and grandsons found carrying on the family craft. Also much trust was placed in these men by their employers: their estimates were asked for and accepted and their bills paid, with few objections raised. All the same, if particular effects were desired, a specialist might be called in to implement local efforts. Sometimes the leading craftsmen of a group might be foreigners or men with experience of elegant undertakings in London. Such were the stuccoists Artari, Bugatti and Serena employed by Chandos at Canons, Cavendish Square and at the Mynd: and Chislo, a plasterer, who was sent to put finishing touches to work at Shaw Hall. Artari and

Serena were also employed at Ditchley on the recommendation of James Gibbs. Plasterers and stuccoists featured largely in the building accounts of the period because their services were needed to produce the effects that current fashion demanded – elaborately decorated ceilings, cornices, wall niches to accommodate pieces of sculpture and mouldings to surround paintings. The recorded details of the designs at Ditchley indicate the precision with which such work was carried out:

> For doing the Basso relives in the Halle, and the Beasts heads with the flowers in the four corners of the Ceiling.
> For doing the four Eagles in the Hall and festoons . . .
> A fine Statuary Frees – curiously carved and enriched with a Lyon and festoons. . . .[3]

The value of the finished product was proved in that the ceiling of each room at Canons was listed and described separately in the Inventory: and that of the Chapel sold, transported and reassembled in the church at Great Witley (Worcestershire) where it can still be seen.

After the plasterers had done their work, additional effects might be added by gilders and painters. Whereas nowadays we are prepared to admire basic design as it stands, 18th century opinion required that both woodwork and plaster should be coloured. Some artists – Laguerre, Francisco and Bellucci for instance – specialised in ceiling and wall paintings and much of their work was incorporated in the rooms at Canons, the Chapel there, and the church of St. Lawrence at Whitchurch, which was included in Chandos's building projects. Other artists, better known perhaps for portraits or history paintings, like Sir Godfrey Kneller, Sir James Thornhill and William Kent, were prepared to use their talents also in embellishing the houses of aristocratic patrons. Chandos would have liked Kneller to paint the staircase at Canons, but such a task was beyond the ageing artist, so it was Thornhill who got the commission. Kent worked for Chandos at Canons and in London: was also responsible for the wall and ceiling decorations at Ditchley: and of course for the well-known (and still remaining) layout of the grounds at Rousham. Lesser unnamed craftsmen presumably gilded and silvered the elaborate cornices in the more important rooms, and decorated bedheads with 'his Grace's arms, a ducal coronet and other elegant ornaments'.

Then there were the carvers and statuaries. Chandos was fortunate in having the means – financial and practical – to secure good materials for his craftsmen to work on, and in not being confined to a choice of English woods or stone to achieve the effects he desired, since through his trading

Ditchley Park

The Hall, Ditchley Park

ventures he had access to supplies of tropical hardwoods and Italian marble which he imported for the making of doors and doorways, presses for books and other library furniture, vases, statues and fireplaces. The latter he considered important: 'I am furnishing my seat and in so doing would have as great a variety of fine chimney pieces as I can get'. Nevertheless, he was not prepared for undue expenditure on these. Having looked at designs of fire-places made in Italy, he decided to import the marble for these but have it worked by English craftsmen whose labour was cheaper. Many of the statues and urns which adorned the outside of Canons were fashioned in lead by John van Nost, who had a yard near Hyde Park Corner where he displayed his goods; and one of his assistants, Charpentiere, 'a man in his time esteemed for his skill, did abundance of works for the Duke' also. But the best known and most skilled of all the carvers who worked for Chandos was Grinling Gibbons, who designed the Chandos memorial to the Duke and his first two wives in the church of St. Lawrence, and was also responsible for one of the Duke's most valued possessions – the carved wooden panel of the Stoning of St. Stephen which hung in his library. Such elaborate carving as that done by Gibbons was of course left unpainted, since its impact depended on the contrasting colours in the woods used, and the three-dimensional effect achieved by the different depths in the carving. The craftsmanship of workers in wood was also apparent in the furnishings of the house. Some of the rooms were 'finely wainscoted with wallnutt tree and mahogany; 'there were walnut and mahogany tables and chairs: in the Library 'a wallnut tree bueroe and a clock in a wallnutt tree viniered Case': and in the Drawing Room a large sideboard table 'inlaid with curious Italian stones and supported by a frame elegantly enriched with figures, festoons, masks, shells and other ornaments richly carved and gilt'.

Another feature of Canons and indeed of other contemporary prestigious houses was an abundance of iron work used both for domestic fixtures and for ornament. Brackets, candleholders, lanterns, candelabra, balustrades, screens and gates might all be made of iron, and at Canons some of the most noteworthy items were considered to be the balustrade of the main staircase, the entrance gates, and the multiplicity of iron screens that separated one part of the garden from another yet 'allowed you to see the whole at once, be you in what Part of the Garden or Parterre you will' (Macky). Following the arrival of the great French ironsmith Jean Tijou, and the popular acclaim of his work in England, men who trained under him were much in demand. Among these was

The Stoning of St Stephen: Carving by Grinling Gibbons

John Montigny, known to be responsible for at any rate some of the iron work at Canons. The minor craftsmen who supplied locks, bolts, hinges and window fitments are not so easily identified, yet it was the attention given to details such as these that helped to produce the overall impression of unique perfection.

Painted walls and ceilings were one source of colour and richness inside Canons. Others were the tapestries, screens, curtains and carpets. Here again Chandos had an advantage over some contemporary builders because his business dealings abroad and family connections had afforded contacts with people in France, Italy, the Low Countries and Turkey, through whom he could obtain materials not generally available in England 'since upon furnishing Canons I am apt to think I shall have occasion for such goods'. Velvet and brocade, silk-lined and fringed, were used for curtains: silk and damask for canopies and bed-hangings. Much of the material was enriched with embroidered birds, trees and flowers on a background of gold and silver thread. White satin was chosen for 'his Grace's bed, most elegantly ornamented and lined with rich green manua', but crimson was favoured for curtains, yellow and green for screens. Furnishings in the Chapel were particularly sumptuous with 'hangings, covers and cushions all in crimson velvet richly laced with gold'. Persian carpets covered the polished wooden floors in all the main rooms.

Finally there were easel pictures, as opposed to those painted directly on to walls and ceilings. Chandos had fallen into the habit of buying paintings as a young man, even before the 18th century dilettanti had established this as a regular and fashionable practice. However, although he knew about established masters and their work, he could not be considered a discriminating buyer nor his collection of paintings one of a uniformly high standard, since many of his purchases were made abroad on the recommendation or at the discretion of relatives and acquaintances who approached Chandos when they heard of pictures that they thought might be of interest to him; or whom Chandos asked to make searches on his behalf. Mathew Decker, Charles Davenant, John Drummond and William Leigh as well as Renier Leers and John Sencerf and other foreign agents were all called on for help in this connection, though their amateur pencil sketches and pieces of string appropriately knotted to indicate sizes cannot have been very effective guides to the quality of the works they were reporting on. Paintings by artists such as Andrea del Sarto, Bellini, Van de Velde and Rubens were among Chandos's acquisitions, and the collection of Raphael's cartoons which hung in the

Saloon among other show-pieces. Religious and mythical themes predominated, but 'flower pieces' adorned the rooms used by Duchess Cassandra. There was a large number of portraits too: of sovereigns and notable public figures, by Van Dyck, Closterman, Peter Lely and Kneller, of the Duke and Duchess and their relatives by Kneller, Mrs. Verelst, Michael Dahl, Jonathan Richardson, Van der Mijn, Charles Jervas and Thomas Hudson. Clearly these painters were recommended by one member of the family to another because the Bourchiers and Leighs who did not live in London or move habitually in fashionable circles, also employed them. Chandos had no artist whom he patronised exclusively or even particularly, as Burlington did with Kent, and Sir Richard Child with Joseph Nollekens, and there are no pictures that help us to visualise the interior of Canons or afford glimpses of the grounds outside, as Hogarth's 'Assembly at Wanstead' does for Lord Castlemaine's dwelling or Zoffany's painting of the Drummonds in their garden at Stanmore. But these two pictures as well as Nollekens' 'Conversation Piece' and Charles Philips's 'Tea Party at Lord Harrington's' do reflect the contemporary taste for such group paintings and the leisurely social life of those portrayed in them.

And what resulted from the money, effort, craftsmanship and artistry that were expended on Canons? In place of a small Tudor manor house, set in a formal garden that conributed little to its significance, there arose a residence, designed as a dominating feature in the landscape, although in comparison with other contemporary mansions it was only moderate in size, 'a square pile, all stone, noble and grand' resembling Ditchley in its compactness rather than Blenheim or Wanstead where winged extensions added considerably to the overall span of the building. As in other houses built for impressing and entertaining important visitors, the ground and first floors at Canons were of equal importance, with spacious rooms lit by high windows, and suitably furnished for the reception and accommodation of both strangers and members of the family. The ground floor was built round a small paved courtyard, glazed over at roof height to afford extra light to the rooms that looked on to it. The main entrance was on the south front of the house via a columned portico that led into the Great Hall 'richly adorned with marbles, statues and bustos' (Vertue). Also on the ground floor were rooms for smoking, billiards, small family gatherings, the Servants' hall, the Dining Room and the Music Room, the latter furnished with a music library and a collection of very fine musical instruments, and large enough to hold the Canons orchestra numbering twenty-four in all, which performed here during meal-times. Access to the first floor was by the great staircase, 'finest by far of any in England, – the steps of marble each of one whole piece, about 22ft in length'. Here, above the Dining Room was the Duke's Library, its ceiling decorated with Bellucci's huge painting of the 'Seven Liberal Arts and Sciences', its furnishings matching the valuable collection of books and folios, astronomical and mathematical instruments housed there. The Long Gallery containing pictures and statues was also on this floor, together with the bedchambers and dressing rooms – all richly appointed – used by the Duke, his family and their guests. The indoor servants, about ninety in number, slept on the attic floor and even their bedrooms had fireplaces, feather beds, chests of drawers, tables and chairs. Key figures in the household, such as the Chaplain, Housekeeper, Director of Music and Gentleman of the Horse also had offices on the ground floor.[4]

As we have noticed, the plumbing facilities at Canons were well ahead of the times, with piped water on two floors, water-closets, marble wash-basins (the 'Beaufett') near the Dining-Room, and a bathing room for the Duke with marble floor, and walls and a stuccoed ceiling. On the whole though, comfort and convenience were sacrificed to effect and one wonders whether meals were ever really hot in view of the distance to be covered between the Kitchen and the Dining Room, and the elaborate procedure that had to be observed by those who carried the dishes and those who supervised them 'till the dishes are sett upon the Table – as every Course is served up.' And how warm and draught-proof were the rooms, in spite of Chandos's orders to his architect to stop the chimneys smoking, and to his Usher 'to take Care good Fires in Winter Time be kept up' in the huge marble fireplaces in all the rooms in use?

Chandos was not unique in having a private chapel and a resident Chaplain attached to his home.: Chatsworth, Blenheim and other places had these too, but the baroque grandeur of the Chapel at Canons (largely reassembled at Great Witley after the demolition of the house in 1747) must have been unusual, with its painted glass windows by Francesco Slater, stuccoed and painted ceiling, and an abundance of richly carved woodwork, a carved and gilt chandelier and a fine organ. The choir and orchestra which performed in the Chapel were also unexpected in a private dwelling, and save for sovereign princes, there can have been few people at any time who commanded the services of such an eminent contemporary musician as Handel. 'Mr. Handel has made me two new anthems, very noble ones and most think they far exceed the two first. He is at work for two more and some overtures to be plaied before the first lesson'. In all, twelve anthems were composed for Chandos, as well as overtures and choral works.[3]

Few also are the private individuals who have undertaken at their own expense the complete rebuilding of a parish church as Chandos did at Whitchurch, on the southern edge of his estate. At the same time as work on Canons was being planned, architect John James was instructed to make a thorough survey of St. Lawrence's and to draw up plans for its rebuilding. The expressed desire that 'the pews should be plac't as they are in cathedrals' and elaborate orders regarding the Brydges gallery to be erected over the west end of the church indicate that even before the attainment of his dukedom Brydges's imagination ranged along grandiose lines. The same artists as were later employed at Canons – Laguerre, Bellucci and Slater – worked on the walls and ceiling; Grinling Gibbons designed the case for the organ and the monument in white marble which dominated the Mausoleum, with its three stately figures – of Chandos flanked by his first two wives, Mary Lake and Cassandra. The altar, cloths for the altar and pulpit, cushions, Bibles and Prayer books, plate and candlesticks were all provided by Chandos. Situated at the end of one of the tree-lined avenues that radiated from Canons itself to its massive entrance gates, the church of St. Lawrence was attended regularly by Chandos and his family, guests and household servants, and was the link between the great house and the surrounding neighbourhood. As he proceeded to services there, flanked by rows of servants, and sat in his gallery looking out over the congregation, the Duke must surely have seen himself as a kind of manorial lord presiding over his court. He referred to St. Lawrence's as 'his' church on occasion, and perhaps this view of himself was strengthened during visits to the Leighs at Adlestrop where the parish church served as a family chapel and burial place, and was in due course to be extensively rebuilt at the Leigh's expense.

Chandos and his fellow builders were the products of their age and contributors to it as well. Their houses reflected their tastes and interests and were the hub of their public and private lives. To the community at large they stood for what was architecturally desirable and reflected the status of their owners. Vertue wrote of Wanstead: 'A noble pile of building, the design of Mr. Campbell, I think much to his reputation, it being great, noble and of fine taste'; while Defoe summed up the achievement of Canons:

> The great palaces in Italy, are either the work of sovereign princes or have been ages in their building. But Canons had not been three

years in the Duke's possession before we saw the prodigy rise out of the ground.

Such descriptions by contemporary writers, and the engravings by Kip, Hulsbergh and others, indicated the wide interest being taken in great houses and a need to satisfy it. That there were among the gentry and aristocracy some who were leading a self-centred existence of little use to any but themselves is undoubtedy true; but there were others who filled administrative posts, especially in local government, who promoted measures for the public good, and who showed consistent benevolence towards all those who served them, were dependent on them in any way, or appealed to them for help. Their households consituted vital factors in local economic life, as Rudder pointed out:

> The inns are well supported by the great travelling through the towns, the shopkeepers and retailers have very considerable dealings with the circumjacent towns and villages who frequent their markets. In most of these (the great landowners) the tradesmen found a valueable customer, the farmer a friend and adviser, and the poor inhabitants hospitality and charity.[6]

Their mansions set in newly laid out gardens and grounds were focal points in the 18th century landscape. According to Defoe:

> Noble seats shine among the trees as Jewels shine in a rich Coronet. They reflect Beauty and Magnificence upon the whole Country and give a kind of character to the Island of Great Britain.

CHAPTER 8

The Management Of Estates And Gardens.

Before James Brydges began to acquire properties in London, generations of his family had been busy consolidating estates in the western counties of Gloucester, Hereford, Radnor and Shropshire, with connections also in Hampshire and Somerset. Advantageous marriages had linked the Brydges with other landowning families in these areas, and the careful management of actual possessions together with the judicious acquisition of more land as it became available, eventually brought considerable areas under their control. In contemporary fashion, the Brydges regarded their estates – whether in the country or in London – as business propositions, only worth while if they brought in considerable rents or were producing consumable and/or saleable goods.

By the 18th century most landowners, and certainly all successful ones, had advanced far beyond the stage of mere subsistence farming; and those who could afford were renting out part of their estates in the country, and investing also in increasingly profitable urban properties from which the rents might be used to finance experiment and improvement elsewhere. Chandos was one of those proprietors who, although obliged to leave much of the practical management of estate business in the hands of stewards, nevertheless kept a close watch on affairs himself, and much of his voluminous correspondence carried on even while he was travelling and away from home, was with his various officials, concerning all aspects of their work, from major decisions to what appear to be rather trivial details. That his stewards remained with him for many years indicated satisfaction on both sides and a considerable degree of confidence and trust between them. It will be remembered that after his sister Katharine Bourchier had been left a widow, Chandos considered that he could best help by offering her the services of his bailiff, who was both knowledgeable in estate affairs and reliable.

Primarily, whether through rents or produce, the purpose of the estates was to ensure Chandos and his family a comfortable standard of living. A regular revenue from rents was, of course, an important adjunct to the salaries afforded by public offices, and a more dependable one than the returns on investments; but in view of the high price of food in London and the spas, produce from the estates was equally valuable. This explains the regular despatch to London from the Brydges estates in the west, of cattle and sheep for meat supplies, hops, grain, cheese, poultry and venison. Chandos claimed and exploited fishing rights on a number of rivers in Herefordshire and Shropshire, and kept his agents in a state of constant alertness against poachers and the erectors of illicit weirs. Herefordshire being the source of 'the richest cider in all Britain', it was natural that much should be made and sent from there to Canons, enough for the household and for Chandos to give away to his friends. His Brydges cousins at Tyberton turned cider-making into a serious business, despatching large quantities 'not too sweet nor yet very harsh' by carrier to an agent in Berkshire, who claimed to have 'noe less than 6 Dukes and Dutchesses and other quality and good company in proportion' all ready to buy Herefordshire's best Red Streak.

Like other thrifty landowners, Chandos was keen to improve the value and output of his estates if opportunities occurred, and was always interested in new ideas, doubtless encouraged in this by his membership of the Royal Society, which since its inauguration in the late 17th century had been doing much to take notice of, and thus set its seal of approval on, progressive experiments in agriculture. In 1728 Chandos was involved in the promotion of an act to legalize the enclosure of common land at Barnet: and since his teamsters and drovers made regular use of the roads between Herefordshire, Radnorshire and London, he favoured the creation of turnpikes on these. In 1728 he consulted his cousin Mr. Westfalling, about the advantage of converting rough ground into a rabbit warren. Evidently they had discussed this subject on a previous occasion and Chandos now wanted facts and figures to convince him of the profitability of such a move: 'I desire you will favour me with the Particulars of your Computations and what charge it will require to make it, supposing it to be the Compass of about 20 or 30 Acres'. Always forward looking, he was aware that arable land needed to be fertilised if its yields were to be increased. Currently all kinds of waste material including rags were being used as manure, and it was a regular practice for the wagons carrying loads of hay from Canons for sale in London stables, to return laden with dung. This was clearly important, as Chandos instructed his agent:

> You'll take care likewise that the Teams as often as they go to London bring constantly back a Load of Dung along with them; they can have no excuse now I think for not doing it, for when I am away there can be no pretence of sending things backwards and forwards from Cannons to London, nor will I allow of any such practices.[1]

The most recent experiment in fertilising agents was with burnt clay, but the limited success of this at Canons drove the Duke to write to a Mr. Hall who had suggested it to him, asking for further particulars:

> My people have been very much in the wrong about it for they have burnt at least ten times the Quantity of Surface you mention. I have burnt 300 loads which I am going to lay on a piece of ground just by the Garden for a Trial.

Livestock too must be kept in good condition, so Henry Perrot was approached:

> Pray did you not tell me that the Mast of the Horse Chestnut if Fried in an Oven and made into a Paste was an excellent feed for Cattle as well as Leys, and that they would grow fat upon it?

Family correspondence contained numerous references to estate business, an indication that this was a topic of unfailing interest; and although Chandos and his London friends might confine their coffee-house talk to investments, trade ventures and foreign news, when travelling round the country and residing on their estates, their attention was quickly switched to the present state of, and future trends in, farming. Neither Chandos nor any of his immediate circle became well-known innovators; nevertheless they were moving with the times, and spoke or wrote of their views and experiences. Seeds 'of severall sortes of Garden Peese and new Turnips' were exchanged with Herefordshire cousins and the merits of stock discussed with the Leighs. Brereton Bourchier sent a well-recommended mare to Canons for breeding purposes: and Henry Perrot was offered 'the deer from the Little Paddock at Shaw' when Chandos disparked it. Visits too, could afford opportunities for observation and may-be new ideas, as a letter from Chandos to Perrot (1735) revealed:

> When I was at Barnsley, I observed you ploughed with Oxen and I think you said you found it abundantly cheaper than with horses. I have a great mind to try the experiment at Canons and shall be

obliged to you if you'll let me know how you manage them – I mean what you give them in the summer, and how you keep them in the winter: how long they generally last you before you put them up to fatten and what quantity of ground, supposing the soil to be a stiff clay, a yoak or two yoak will be able to Plough in a day. I take it for granted you are obliged to house them in the winter, but I suppose you give them no corn and only a little hay: and pray let me know what they will cost a Yoak and if there are any to be bought fit for the purpose about you. I reckon in the summer nightes they ly out all night in some or other of the grounds.[2]

The exchange of animals between friends and their movement between one estate and another merely added to the already regular passage of livestock along the roads leading to London where the markets for cattle, sheep and poultry could never be satisfied. A letter from Chandos to his steward in 1735, as well as illustrating co-operation between estates, also paints a vivid picture of the trade in turkeys between East Anglia and the capital:

If due care is not taken we shall lose the opportunity of buying the Turkies . . . they come up before this time of the year and I dare say if the Bayliff went over to Lord Tylney's Bayliff at Wanstead and desired him to secure a matter of 30 out of the first droves that went by (for most of them come up the Essex road) he would not fail to do it; tho' I can't imagine why I can't have them as they pass through Edgware and Barnet, for I am sure some drovers must before this have gone by.[3]

Yearly crops of grain and fruit and gains from livestock were the obvious and immediate returns on land, but the really businesslike owner was anxious to exploit every potentiality of his estate. Thus Chandos concerned himself with making as much as he could out of the timber supplies on his land. The amount felled each year was to be strictly limited: 'I hope there is not mistake this year in the quantity of ground that has been cut as there was two or three years ago, when without my knowledge, there was 15 acres instead of 10 cut down' For furniture and decorative effects, the fashion was turning from English oak and Baltic pine to tropical hardwoods, but home produced woods – elm, beech, sycamore, lime, ash – were still in demand for building purposes, tools, farming implements, hop-poles and fuel. Letters exchanged with his agent at Shaw showed that Chandos was aware of what his woods should be producing and how much it was worth; and anxious that the men who cut the timber should not claim higher wages than they were entitled to, nor take more in the way of perquisites than was their due. He was also alive to the importance of ensuring supplies for future use, and in addition to introducing many elms and oaks into the grounds at Canons, wrote to Perrot for instructions as to how to plant some of his Inclosures with fir-trees, 'now that the rain has softened the ground'. Tree-planting, both for utilitarian and ornamental purposes was very much in vogue. John Evelyn had advised landowners 'to adorn their demesnes with trees of venerable shade and profitable timber', and this precept had been put into practice by private individuals and professional gardeners such as Stephen Switzer, George London and Henry Wise. Duchess Cassandra's father, Frances Willoughby, had tried to replace timber on his estates lost during the Civil Wars, by planting innumerable acorns; Sir Josiah Child had made avenues of walnut trees a feature of his grounds at Wanstead; and Chandos's contemporaries the Duke of Beaufort at Badminton and Lord Bathurst at Cirencester achieved fame by the extent of their tree planting, designed to produce an impressive layout in the present, and resources of timber for estate use and for sale in the future.

Even with those parts of the estate near enough to the house to be accounted 'the garden', although the element of pleasure was foremost when plans were being made, it still seemed desirable that usefulness too should be served: that orchards, greenhouses and espaliers should produce fruit for the table, the Kitchen Garden vegetables, and the Physic Garden herbs to supply remedies to stock the still-room shelves. Fish ponds contained some edible species, and the poultry yard a source of eggs and table birds. Nevertheless, in respect of the ground nearest the house, artistic considerations took precedence over the scientific and economic, and those who strolled along the terraces enjoyed walking along shady avenues, and admired the elaborate fountains and lakes in the gardens of the early 18th century, were probably not aware that all these were part of the overall plan for the estate. In paying as much attention as he did to the layout and embellishment of the grounds at Canons and Shaw Hall, Chandos was at one with contemporaries, as for instance Sir Richard Child, Lord Bathurst, Lord Burlington, Lord Lichfield and many others; and like them he was greatly influenced by current writing on horticulture and engravings of garden plans; undoubtedly too he was driven on by his desire to make the approaches and surroundings contributory to the perfection of his houses. In London and Bath, his building projects were essentially urban and had neither space nor need for elaborate gardens; but at Shaw Hall on a small scale and Canons on a larger one, he consciously strove to incorporate in his plans all the currently fashionable features – fountains and canals, avenues of trees, statues, urns filled with flowers, shrubs in pots, and contrived vistas of the grounds from the house, and of the house from the grounds.

Where grounds and gardens were concerned, Duchess Cassandra had definite views and preferences. While travelling with her brother during the 1690's and early years of the 18th century, she had visited a number of newly built mansions and surveyed their surroundings critically; she had also helped her brother to replan the grounds of their family home at Wollaton. Badminton and Boughton, Wilton and Longleat, seem to have impressed her most, the former for the scale of the tree-planting, and the latter for the effects obtained through the elaborate use of water; and it was a scheme commensurate with the grand scale of these that Chandos embarked on at Canons, and to a lesser extent at Shaw Hall. At neither place was the permanent outdoor staff unduly large. Shaw had a head gardener, with two men and a weeding woman under him; while at Canons, the workers were assigned in groups to particular parts of the garden – the Parterre, the Greenhouse garden and the Kitchen garden. Some of these might be deployed elsewhere from time to time, to rake gravel, weed paths or clear obtrusive shoots from the boles of elm trees; but while the grounds were being laid out and large undertaking were involved, extra labour had to be taken on. John Hore the canal engineer who planned and directed the waterworks at Shaw, needed considerable extra help to clear an existing canal of reeds, and to tap the river Lambourn in order to fill another newly made canal, and facilitate the introduction of a cascade. At Canons, where reservoirs had to be dug to supply several newly made lakes, fishponds and ornamental canal below the terrace along the south front of the house, as many as 46 men were used at a time to remove mud and carry away rubbish. For weeding, raking and lighter work, women were employed at Canons, being paid at half the rate of the men – eightpence as compared with one shilling and threepence a day. The week was a 6-day one, but one person was engaged 'for watching on Sundays' – at a mere sixpence a day. The regular outdoor staff, about 40 in all, had their own quarters near the Kitchen Garden. In charge of the waterworks was Dr. Desaguliers, who combined theological knowledge with engineering expertise, though seemingly more concerned with exercising the latter than in fulfilling his spiritual commitments to the congregation of St. Lawrence's, Whitchurch.

Just as the Royal Works had helped to promote professional architects, so the elaboration and improvement of royal gardens had encouraged an interest in new designs, new plantings, new effects. Charles II, completely won over by what he had seen of the work of Le Nôtre in France, and William III devoted to the formality of Dutch gardens, set in motion a fashion for the aristocracy and gentry to follow, by appointing gardeners to undertake work in St. James's Park, at Kensington and Hampton Court. The favour of Queen Anne established the reputation of Henry Wise, who with his partner George London ran the nationally famous nursery at Brompton, and was consulted by landowners from all over the country about new plans for their estates. Brompton, though perhaps the best known, was only one of several nurseries in the London area which supplied an advisory service, and fulfilled the demands of enthusiatic gardeners for a wide range of plants; and the size and particularity of some of the orders would seem impressive even in these days. By the early 18th century, nurserymen were able to supply not merely indigenous species, but plants from abroad as well, so that North American evergreens, Mediterranean fruits and Dutch bulbs could all be found in their lists. By comparison with modern standards prices were not expensive, and occasioned no surprise even with the additional cost of packing in moss, matting or baskets, carriage and turnpike dues. Most of the lists offered an astonishing variety of trees, shrubs, herbaceous plants and seeds, but there were also stockists who specialised in particular lines, as for instance Mr. Cross 'at the sign of the Orange Trees in Cecil Street in the Strand where orange trees are sold for a crown a peice both bigg and small, soe that you may have wch you like best'.

In due course many of the garden makers were able to produce much of what they needed in the way of new stocks from their own greenhouses and nurseries. Chandos had hothouses at both Shaw Hall and Canons, and for heating the latter imported 10,000 turfs specially from Holland, having required his nephew William Leigh to obtain instructions as to how they might be used most economically, since

> it requires above 30 to keep a fire in for 24 hours in a stove, that is to heat a hothouse for raising of foreign plants, where as I think you wrote me word that 12 or 14 would do that service in Holland.

Here were produced the pineapples for which Canons was well known, the friends who received these as presents being asked to return the tops for further propagation. Nursery beds too were useful, and most large estates boasted these – Blenheim, Badminton, Longleat for instance, and

Management of Estates and Gardens

Ditchley where in one month (November 1740) two workmen were employed in 'tacking up 14060 young Elms out of ye nursery and planting of them in ye Platoons'. Similarly at Canons in 1721 there were enough young elms in the nursery for planting out in lines three deep along the avenue to St. Lawrence's, Whitchurch and beyond, nearly three miles in all.

A further source of material for their gardens was the regular exchange of plants and seeds between fellow-landowners. Addison made gentle fun of Will Wimble who was apt to be found carrying a tulip root in his pocket from one friend to another, but this in fact was what did happen and explains the gradual spread of unusual species, as cuttings and roots were established and then used for further propagation. Chandos was especially fortunate in being able to engage agents of the trading companies in Africa as well as friends and acquaintances in America and the West Indies to obtain plants for him. All these seem to have been optimistic in the extreme, to judge by the number of plants despatched and how many were lost in transit. As Duchess Cassandra wrote to Mrs Dunbar in Antigua:

> The plants which you took the trouble of sending have suffered so much in the journey that I doubt they will never recover it; such of these with many heads (which are very curious) I never saw before; of the single sort of Turks Heads, we have had several, but in regard they are but annuals and can't be preserved here a second year.

It was also quite usual for head gardeners to be allowed to exchange roots and seeds with their opposite numbers on other estates, provided that their employers did not suffer and they themselves did not profit by the transactions. The question of the rights and obligations of head gardeners raises an interesting point. In December 1729, a letter written by Chandos's secretary to the gardener at Shaw observed:

> There are several Payments for Tools bought for the use of the Garden; as far as anything of this kind is done, there should be an Inventory made which the Gardener should sign, acknowledging that he has those several goods in his Custody, promising to deliver them to his Grace's Order, wear and tear excepted.

Seemingly at this point there was no contract between Chandos and his head gardeners, and one would like to know whether he was out of the ordinary or not in this, since not many years later we find members of the Leigh family signing very detailed agreements with their gardeners as regards the duties they were expected to perform and the extent of their rights and resposibilities. Only 'extraordinary accidents arising from Tempests' or other remote causes exempted them from liability for the satisfactory state of tools and the garden generally, and on all occasions they were to be 'punctual to Family hours and Subservient to the Rules thereof' – a point which Chandos himself would surely have approved.

Fauna as well as flora adorned the grounds at Canons. Deer had been used as a decorative feature in parks for a long while before this, and even sheep, cattle, geese and swans could contribute to the interest of the landscape. But the increasing awareness and availability of rare exotic creatures in the 18th century, tempted wealthy landowners to add these to the attractions of their pleasure gardens. Earlier, during her journeys, Duchess Cassandra had been to Wrest Park where 'tame Fowl and Pheasants' in special enclosures might be seen and fed by visitors; and game birds, brought from Herefordshire, were also on show at Canons, along with 'Bruxelles Fowls', a present from Henry Perrot:

> They all came very well except that one of the Hens was crampt in the feet upon the journey but it is like to do well again. They are very beautiful birds and I am much obliged to you for them.

But even more interesting and unusual were the storks, flamingoes, parrots and giant tortoises imported from the West Indies, which Chandos was apparently always ready to receive. A letter to Mr. Potter, an African Company agent, in 1723, contained a fairly wide (but not completely unlimited) brief:

> If you meet with any Rarities of Birds, Fowl for Ponds, Deer of a small size or such curios (but no Lyons or Tygers or Beasts of Prey) I shall be obliged to you if you'll send 'em over.

Finally, the work of man was brought in to ensure that Art surpassed Nature. At the time, fashion dictated that garden buildings, statues and other artifacts should be introduced to adorn the grounds of great houses being modernised and improved. Talman had designed a graceful orangery for William Blathwayt at Dyrham and was to produce a similar building at Wanstead for Sir Richard Child, in both cases dovetailing his plans with those of George London, who was responsible for the layout of paths, bowling green, lawns and other features. A mock mediaeval castle and other fanciful buildings added interest to Lord Bathurst's park at Cirencester, and Ditchley too had several pavilions. Although London had provided ideas for Canons just before his death, the actual work

Cirencester House and Park

there was carried out by one of his followers Tilleman Brobart, but Chandos does not seem to have favoured buildings in his grounds, and except for a summer-house did not indulge in these. There was however no lack of other man-made ornaments. Brick pillars, decorated with leopards bearing the Chandos arms and capped with oil lamps, lined the avenues leading from the main gates to the house: scattered throughout the grounds in eye-catching positions were statues of classical figures: and in full view of Chandos's Library windows stood an equestrian statue of George I by John van Nost, its specially turfed site surrounded by railings. Commissioned works in stone and lead by known sculptors, as well as ready-made pieces exhibited in London yards were reasonably easy to come by, since supply had expanded to meet increasing demand. The effect of such statuary in a landscape can still be seen as it was originally in Kent's layout at Rousham; elsewhere as at Canons it has been transformed or disappeared entirely because of changing tastes and circumstances. In fact Chandos never had 'statues thick as trees', nor 'trees cut to statues' as Pope accused him of doing; however, some of the statues and the urns which lined the terraces and walks were gilded and painted and so must have given an impression of colourfulness and pageantry to the whole place.

Of all his houses, Canons was the only one that Chandos threw open to the public. His properties in the western counties were mostly tenanted: those in Bath, when not being used by himself or his family, were rented to other visitors to the spa: Shaw Hall was always regarded as essentially a private dwelling. Canons however, rather like Blenheim, was a symbol of status, designed to be seen and expected to be put on show. Within travelling distance of London it was an attraction, as was Wanstead, to those who wanted an objective for an excursion different from the more routine visits to pleasure gardens or wells. It was also listed among the great houses to be visited by the 'professional' travellers such as Defoe and Macky, and considered important enough for events there to be chronicled regularly in the press – as for instance, the theft of goods from St. Lawrence's church, the opening of Canons Chapel accompanied by the strains of Handel's music, the delivery of large quantities of building stone, the visits of some eminent politicians or foreign potentates.

Such publicity, which satisfied those who wanted to be informed of the latest social events and architectural developments, also provided the satirists and those who disapproved of pomp and show with grounds for their criticism of Chandos. All the same, for whatever reason, it brought visitors to Canons where, during the 1720's and early 1730's the business

Canons: Entrance Porch

Canons: Garden Urn

of opening to the public resembled that of one of the stately homes of today. There were four entrances to the grounds, each guarded by lodges where Chandos's pensioners lived as gatekeepers. The two main approaches from Whitchurch and Edgware converged on the south and east sides of the house, so that from a distance the angle of the building merged with the neighbouring walls to give an impression of greater size than was the case. The visitor passed through wrought iron entrance gates adorned with ducal coronets, exchanging the unmade surface of the high road for the well-raked and weed-free, gravelled walks that led through the grounds. The south approach from Whitchurch was paved at the start and encircled a large brass sundial en route. Throughout the estate there was marked evidence of the careful attention given to land and trees, and to the livestock that grazed in the park or added colour and interest to the lakes and fountain pools.

Near the house, open-parkland gave way to formal lawns (mown and weeded two or three times a week), parterres and flower borders, and then steps led up to the terraces and entrances to the building. The western approach was via a courtyard round which the domestic offices, storerooms and stables were situated: and the Kitchen and Physic Gardens were on the west and north sides of the house. That fees for visiting Canons were profitable is indicated by their being linked in the household accounts to specific purposes – for the payment of gardeners, of extra maids needed for cleaning the house, of the cost of cleaning materials and repairs; and not surprisingly there was a certain amount of rivalry between the head gardener and the housekeeper as to the allocation of benefits from the returns of showing people round. Unlike some places which had definite opening times, determined on a class basis – noblemen and gentlemen being admitted on different days from 'other people' Canons seems to have been generally accessible except on Sundays. We do not know to what extent those who showed the visitors round were plagued with crowds and silly questions, nor whether they conformed to 'the laudable custom of England that they should be unacquainted with what they were showing', but it does seem as if pilfering may have been a problem, since in 1735, Chandos ordered his steward to make a careful inventory of the goods at Canons, so that a practice in operation elsewhere might be introduced here:

> I observed when I was at the Duke of Devonshire's, the Duke of Leeds's and the Duke of Kingston's a very good method which I intend shall be the same in my house viz that in every room there

was a paper pinned up against the hangings or chairs containing particulars of all the Furniture in that Room, so that the least part thereof could at any time be discovered if missing.'

By the time that Chandos thought of introducing this regulation, Canons had lost its novelty appeal for tourists, and the numbers anxious to view the house and gardens were falling off. As we shall see, the circumstances of Chandos's personal life were changing also, but in any case, new ideas in building and in gardening were already being promoted by a new generation of patrons, so that the formal grandeur of Canons no longer seemed the acme of perfection; instead it was classical restraint in building and the natural landscaping of gardens that was earning approval. Unlike many other establishments that were adapted to suit changing tastes during the course of the 18th century, when perforce Canons was put on the market after Chandos's death in 1744, its purchaser – William Hallett – made no attempt to retain and modify the building; except for the cellar, the whole house was pulled down and a new Canons erected 'not very extensive – an elegant and compact residence', very different from 'the magnificent Palace' of its former owner. And the grounds, previously 'adorned with grand decorations in the Taste of the Times' were judiciously modelled into a pleasing Park. Its outstanding features – the canals, basins, broad walks and parterres were too much rooted in the French style of the past to please the 18th century English gentleman anxious to assert his national distinction and independence by realising the ideals imbued in him by his classical education and Italian travels. Now Nature and the 'Genius of the Place' must be consulted and spontaneous beauties aimed at, as if the gardener painted as he planted. The compartmented arrangement of the grounds at Canons, outlined by iron railings and emphasised by contrasts between flower-beds and gravel paths, lawns and shrubberies and paved terraces and open parkland, all laid out with the precision of a draughtsman, gave way to the picturesque ebb and flow of landscaping where 'half the skill is decently to hide' and 'parts answering parts should *slide* into the whole'.

That his successor at Canons claimed to be improving the estate 'both in Beauty and Value' implied not only that Chandos's adornment of his property had been at fault but that his management of it had not been economically profitable either.

CHAPTER 9

The 1730's And After

In some ways the achievement of a dukedom marked the peak of Chandos's career. Socially it was unlikely that he would rise further: and he had already given up the idea of taking political office again or playing a leading part in national affairs, although there is no doubt that he still enjoyed having contact with the court and leading political figures like Sir Robert Walpole, and being in a position to make informed comments on the current situation. Financially, his fortunes fluctuated according to the progress or otherwise of trading companies and other ventures. As we have seen, the major disaster of the early 1720's – the South Sea Bubble – did not affect Chandos as much as some, but he did lose money in this, also through his investments in the Royal African Company and the York Building Company; and his personal ventures into mining, building and the development of Bridgwater, even if they had been successful, could never have brought him a fortune commensurate with the one he had made at the Paymaster's Office. This meant that during the 1720's his income was not expanding to meet the increasing cost of maintaining a ducal standard of living, and that he had to think of balancing his budget as opposed to spending indiscriminately.

Duchess Cassandra claimed that her husband never allowed her to go short of money, and certainly during the 1720's no worthy request for help from relatives or friends was denied by Chandos or his wife. In spite of the large number of her letters that has been preserved, we have none of Cassandra's account books and almost no indication of her personal tastes in clothes or jewels. Her husband's purchases of materials for her trousseau before their marriage – 'not too gay and airy' – would seem to indicate that she was not fond of anything gaudy or extravagant; and there is no record of his buying expensive jewels for her nor of her wearing them (vide her portraits), so she evidently made no exceptional demands on his pocket during their marriage. For the rest, careful management of his estates and meticulous attention to the details of their household economy at Canons kept Chandos's affairs reasonably stable.

During the 1730's the situation changed somewhat, so that carefulness developed into stringent economy, and odd petty meannesses became more overt ways of saving money. Some of the properties in Herefordshire and Hampshire and the house in St. James's Square were sold: new ventures more warily undertaken and more quickly abandoned if not immediately and obviously promising. And for the first time, we find the Duchess apologising to members of the family for being unable to help them as liberally as in former years. In the house at Canons the number of servants was gradually cut down, and food supplies more strictly controlled than before; and throughout Chandos's estates even greater emphasis was laid on efficiency and the profitable sale of produce. For instance the Duke displayed chagrin and was inclined to suspect sharp practice on the part of gardeners when the yield of peat at Shaw Hall failed to come up to expectations; and he was bitterly disappointed when attempts to grow herbs and grapes there (for sale at a profit) ended in dismal failure. However, it was not just material circumstances that began to weigh heavily on Chandos. Possibly after the achievement of his dukedom and completion of Canons, life began to seem something of an anti-climax with no further soaring ambitions to fire his enthusiasm; and while less demanding physically and nervously, it was certainly less stirring mentally for the quiet enjoyment of music, books and pictures to constitute a major part of life instead of merely the adjunct to an eventful daily routine.

Family affairs, too, during this period, were a source of sadness and disappointment to Chandos. Firstly, in 1735, Duchess Cassandra died, rather suddenly in spite of the fact that she had never enjoyed really good health. Throughout her life she had pushed illness into the background, ignoring it when possible, making light of it when defeated and obliged to take to her bed; and although her visits to Tunbridge Wells and Bath with her husband had been undertaken with the hope of gaining relief from distressing symptoms, this fact never obtruded itself into the letters she wrote at such times. Her death on July 17th from apoplexy came after a period of better health and was therefore more of a shock to Chandos, whom she had left to go on a short visit to some Brydges cousins at Mill Hill; and there is no doubt that for a while Chandos was shattered by it. 'He lost in her a Lady of the most exemplary and exalted Virtues as rendered her an Honour to her Sex and an Ornament to the British nation' reported the *Gentleman's Magazine*. He was much older than when he had lost his first wife; also, unlike Cassandra, he was hypochondriacal where his health was concerned, and he now had to face life and possible illness without an understanding, comforting partner at his side to calm his fears and keep things in proportion for him. According to a letter written at the time to Henry Perrot, all the places where he had been with Cassandra were unbearable to him. 'Somewhere I must go into the country for the air, and Cannons and Shaw I hate the thought and dread the sight of. Adieu dear Sir, and may you enjoy all the happiness this world can give which is now taken away from me.'

Duchess Cassandra was buried in the tomb which had been prepared for her in the church of St. Lawrence. When the latter was being rebuilt, Chandos had had a monument room erected against the north aisle to contain the tombs and memorials of his family, together with the monument designed for himself and his two wives. By 1735, the room was already overcrowded, so after Cassandra's death, Chandos had it redesigned and enlarged – James Gibbs was called in again for advice – to allow for more burials and make it possible for the front of his own tomb to be moved forward leaving a space for coffins behind. Two craftsmen, Henry Cheere, a statuary, and Gaetano Brunetti, a painter, new to Canons but already fashionable in London, were engaged to complete the decoration of the new room. Although possibly not all the work on the monument had been done by Grinling Gibbons when it was first made in 1717, he certainly designed it and carved the figures. (To judge by the letters that passed between him and Chandos at the time, the latter was not altogether pleased with the carving, but it may have been Gibbons's charges that he objected to, rather than his work.) The monument, though not outstanding, is definitely effective and impressive, and has recognisable likenesses of Mary Lake and Cassandra in the figures kneeling at each side of the Duke, here shown in senatorial guise, calmly confident of his role and position.

After Cassandra's burial, Chandos set out on a tour of parts of the country he had never visited before, curiously enough taking in some of the great houses and gardens that Cassandra had seen being renovated over thirty years earlier – Wrest, Kiveton and Boughton for instance. Then he spent several weeks with his nephew William Leigh at hospitable Adlestrop, whence he visited Blenheim, Heythrop and Ditchley. He moved on from there to his other nephew Henry Perrot at Barnsley, and thence after a short visit to Shaw Hall back to London. Here the idea of marrying again suggested itself, when he resumed a former friendship with Lydia Davall, a widow of long standing with a fortune of £40,000 and several London properties, though, to be fair, it was much more her capacity for companionship than her assets that led Chandos to make her his third wife.

The marriage ceremony took place in strict privacy on April 13th 1736, and a short honeymoon was spent at Canons. The new Duchess was twenty years younger than her husband, attractive, good tempered, and both willing and able to adapt her ways to Chandos's needs and inclinations. Before long they moved back to London to take up residence in the new house in Cavendish Square which had become ready for habitation only just before Cassandra's death. Chandos's attention to the final stages of the decorations reveal a spark of his old enthusiasm for having the best craftsmen available to plaster the ceilings and decorate the walls; and as he still had contacts at Court and business in the City, the new house quickly became a useful base as St. James's Square and previous residences had been. For a while the Duke and his new Duchess continued to use Shaw Hall as a refuge, but he was becoming disenchanted with it and in due course allowed Lord Caernarvon to take up residence there for a while.

Meanwhile, in other personal aspects, life was proving disappointing for Chandos. The marriage of his niece Martha to Henry Perrot, of which he and Duchess Cassandra hoped so much, had broken down, and increasing ill-health was taking Perrot abroad quite a lot and depriving Chandos of a ready confidant. The affection was still there, but correspondence was necessarily less than regular while Perrot was travelling to various spas in search of cures for his ailments; and although Martha and her two daughters were still in England, Chandos seems to have had no direct contact with them.

A source of much greater disappointment however, was his son Henry, Lord Caernarvon, in whom marriage, membership of Parliament and office in the household of the Prince of Wales had all failed to induce maturity, sobriety and a sense of responsibility. Chandos was driven from irritation to exasperation by Henry's failure to exploit the opportunities afforded by his position at Court, but nothing seemed to stir him out of his apathetic attitude, and the only noticeable result of his association with the heir to the throne was an increased propensity for living beyond his means. Time and time again Chandos was obliged to pay outstanding debts for clothes, entertainments and wagers on horses, in order to extricate his son from trouble; and meanwhile the latter was living largely at Chandos's expense, in his houses at Cavendish Square and Shaw Hall, and drawing upon Canons for domestic supplies. In the end, even his father's family pride and stubborn hopes were defeated by

Lydia, Lady Davall, 2nd Duchess of Chandos

Anne Jefferies, 3rd Duchess of Chandos

The 1730's and After 161

Henry's refusal to face facts, as Chandos wrote in a letter to a nephew, Colonel Inwood:

> I am heartily sorry to find by what you write, the news I heard of Lord Caernarvon's taking another house, to be true; (I wonder) how it is possible for him to imagine he can live anything near within compass; and it is strange that after having felt the inconveniences of being in debt, he would not rather choose to live on bread and water than bring himself under the same circumstances again.[1]

Chandos and Duchess Cassandra until she died, were also very much concerned about Caernarvon's children, Caroline and James, whom they often had to stay with them, rather than allowing them to be left in the care of servants[2] when Caernarvon's attendance on the Prince of Wales took him and his wife to Windsor, St. James's or Newmarket. Their mother, Mary, features very little in the family papers and seems to have had almost no influence over her husband; indeed, being gentle and affectionate, she may often have been hurt by his inconsiderate ways. Chandos considered 'a better woman nor a more tender wife, I believe no man was ever blessed with', and when Mary died of consumption in August 1738, he employed Henry Cheere to prepare her monument in the Chandos mausoleum at St. Lawrence's, and asked his nephew Dr. Theophilus Leigh to compose her epitaph. Meanwhile Caernarvon lost little time in looking for another wife. His letters, and presumably his attitude, to women friends and acquaintances tended to be flippant and flirtatious, so it is not surprising that some outrageous stories were told, and believed, about his second marriage to Anne Jefferies. That she was bought from her ostler husband at the Pelican Inn at Newbury was not beyond the bounds of possibility where Caernarvon was concerned, but his new wife's demeanour, and subsequent behaviour certainly belied an uneducated and inelegant background. However, for some reason, the marriage was kept secret at the time (1740), and not celebrated publicly until after the death of Chandos in 1744, although it is a mystery in itself how the situation could have been hidden from the latter so successfully, especially as he himself was doing his best, after 1738, to find another wife for Caernarvon.

Less of a source of anxiety was the family of Chandos's elder son John. The Dowager Marchioness of Caernarvon, Catherine, and her daughters Catherine and Jane, were financially well off thanks to a satisfactory marriage settlement and the continuing generosity of Catherine's parents, especially her mother, Lady Dysart, who when she died in 1740 left a fortune of £30,000 to Catherine in trust for her daughters. Views of the Dowager Marchioness are difficult to reconcile. Chandos evidently thought well of her and left her fifty guineas in his will 'as a token of my sincere esteem and respect for her and of my thankfulness to her for the great care she hath taken of my two granddaughters and the tenderness she hath constantly shewn them'. But others, with a certain malicious glee, related accounts of her outbursts of temper, and irrational uncontrolled behaviour which could turn her almost instantly from an affectionate mother into a jealous virago. Both daughters escaped her tantrums in the end, but not before they had been subjected to many public humiliations. On one occasion Lady Jane, the more submissive of the two, having kept a long-fixed social engagement against an objection raised at the last minute by her mother, returned home to find herself locked out and denied admittance: and having taken refuge with her sister, was pursued by a stream of vituperative and threatening messages carried by embarrassed, terrified servants. Not surprisingly, such stories were embroidered in the telling and other more apochryphal ones added to the saga, such as the rumour that Lady Jane had eloped with and married a footman. In fact she did marry, but quite conventionally and most satisfactorily, her cousin James, son of Chandos's brother Henry and next in succession to the Chandos title should anything happen to Caernarvon's heir, Lord Wilton – a fact which explains the important place he held in the affections of his uncle, who obtained a commission for him in the navy and followed his career and activities during the early years of the Austrian Succession War, with mixed anxiety and pride.

As the 1730's progressed, Chandos – now in his sixties – must have felt that he was losing touch with much that was going on. The death of close friends and relatives with whom he had corresponded regularly and confidentially, deprived him of a source of sympathy and reassurance; his income, which despite all efforts to inflate it, failed to expand to meet any further aggrandisement of his life style; and his health was a constant source of anxiety to him. To judge by their letters, a great many people during the 18th century were obsessed with the topic of health, or rather ill-health, for the symptoms, diagnosis, progress and treatment of all kinds of diseases were solemnly reported. Although she rarely commented on her own health, Duchess Cassandra was prepared to discuss that of other people and to recommend remedies to them. Chandos was much readier to mention his imagined and actual ailments, and keen both to hear of other people's remedies and to share his own. Quite large amounts of mineral water were sent to him from Bristol, Bath and

Lady Jane and Lady Catherine Brydges

Lord Wilton, Grandson of Chandos

The 1730's and After

overseas spas, and in turn he supplied bottles of water from the London spas to his friends and family. A letter to Henry Perrot ran:

> The Duchess of Chandos . . . desires me to tell you she has heard such great commendation of a Mineral water at Lambeth and can depend upon the truth of these Accounts so much, and of their great virtue in Cancerous cases, that she wishes my Sister could be prevailed on to try 'em if she will, wee will send her down 6 bottles every week; if she drinks a quart in the day, it's as much as anybody takes.[3]

Chandos found his failing eyesight a very real affliction since it affected everything that he wanted to do, and any worsening in the state of his eyes cast him into despondency and even despair. The conflicting advice of various doctors did nothing to dispel his fears or ease the symptoms and served merely to drive him into trying the remedies suggested by acquaintances such as his wine merchant or the aged mother of his secretary. The muddled thinking of both professionals and amateurs was reflected not only in the substances prescribed (e.g. viper's fat) but in the varying opinions as to how they should be used, Portugese snuff for instance might be either snuffed up *or* put into the eyes.

But it was not only in his personal circumstances that Chandos found himself in the midst of change. The political situation too was not as it had been when, as a young man about town, he had embarked on a public career, seizing every opportunity that occurred to further his ambitions. In spite of having deliberately chosen a secondary role after 1719, he was nevertheless still active, continuing to put in attendance at Court, lending support to debates in the House of Lords, serving as Lord Lieutenant, and remaining on friendly terms with some of the ministers, and in particular, Sir Robert Walpole. Moreover, in spite of stating that he no longer had influence in governmental circles or with prominent people, the fact that he was approached and asked for favours indicated that he was still in the public eye; and results showed that he was still in a position to secure promotion in the Navy, both for his nephew Jemmy and the son of a cousin George Rodney: and to obtain the position of organist at the Charterhouse for his former Director of Music, Dr. Pepusch, and a place in the school for his godson James Rodney. As the 1730's drew to a close however, even the all-powerful Walpole had passed the peak of his success, having lost his closest ally at Court when Queen Caroline died in 1737, and being under attack in Parliament from an opposition led by William Pitt, angered by Walpole's methods of holding on to power and no doubt jealous at the success of these. The long period of peace which had enabled the Hanoverians to be accepted as sovereigns of England – thus keeping the Whigs in power and ensuring that the Tories remained in political exile – was coming to an end; and when at the sight of Captain Jenkin's severed ear, the Commons clamoured for revenge and the declaration of war on Spain, Walpole was forced to submit.

Chandos had a fatalistic attitude to the prospect of the future: 'If we enter not into a war, we shall be rendered contemptible to the last degree, and if we do 'tis ten thousand to one but we are undone', but he still believed that Walpole was the only man who could steer the country through such a crisis (as he had during the South Sea Bubble) though Walpole himself knew that the change of policy might well bring about his downfall. At the same time, those who had benefited from his friendship or profited from the political climate he had created, would also be at a loss; and in showing genuine concern for Walpole's health and his political status during the last precarious years of his ministry (1739-1742) Chandos too was acknowledging an awareness of the passing of a period during which members of the governmental classes had waxed rich on the fruits of office and directed the affairs of the country in such a way as to maintain a status quo favourable to their own interests.

Economically too, the speed and degree of change was being intensified as the business world became more competitive, and increasingly singleness of purpose and ruthlessness were required of those who committed themselves to it. The gentleman amateur might well preserve his status by dabbling in investments, agricultural improvements or industrial ventures, but he could not hope to hold his own, let alone prevail successfully against those for whom business was in the blood or perforce had become second nature as the only means of survival. Chandos was always anxious to come off best in his business deals, and so was frequently suspected of sharp practice and treated accordingly. That he did not in fact resort to dishonesty while his counterparts did so, therefore dismayed and disconcerted him; nor did he ever learn from experience.

The pace of life too, was for the young and confident, and could not be maintained by one as old and uncertain as Chandos. One by one his investments were sold off or realised, and he became increasingly reluctant to take an interest in new schemes. Even those he did favour, e.g. turnpikes and enclosures – had worrying repercussions that he was at a loss to cope with, since his instinctive kindness of heart pulled him in a different direction from his dutiful belief in the need to preserve the peace of the country at all costs. For the rapidly expanding population of England no longer fitted into the ordered class structure of earlier centuries, but was a mobile, changing community impossible to categorise either by class or calling, and at variance with the hierarchical principles which had been the guiding lines of Chandos's social and economic thinking.

> Indeed the pains which has been taken of late years to infuse notions of liberty in the minds of the populace has been so successfull that they become every day more and more possess't with an opinion that they are not only not to be slaves, but that they ought to be masters.

The Duke was neither arrogant nor cruel in his attitude, but his continuing belief in the effectiveness of paternal benevolence as a solution to social distress proved that he lacked the perception and experience to understand the scale of the factors that were to become inescapable problems during the remaining decades of the century and beyond. A bad harvest in 1739, followed by the biting cold of a winter that even the fires of Canons could not keep at bay, made him aware that 'the condition of the lower sort of people must be rendered very hard and miserable' and prompted an order that all the poor of Edgware and on his other estates should be supplied with beef and bread at his expense from January to March; but already so localised and limited a measure of relief was an anachronism.

Chandos's reaction to increasing pressures and challenges was to retreat into private life. During the later 1730's and early 1740's he remained at Canons or Cavendish Square for the winter months and did not travel, since he and Duchess Lydia both felt the cold. Visits to Bath and Radnorshire were given up completely, and necessary business connected with properties there conducted through correspondence with stewards. Only journeys to Shaw Hall in summer continued, where friends from neighbouring shires might join the household and pass the time in domestic pleasures – conversation, games of chess, backgammon and whist, sedate walks round the ground. Rather naturally, the Duke now turned to the younger generation to keep him in touch with current happenings. His two grandchildren, Caroline and James, Lord Wilton, were still regular visitors to Canons, and Chandos took an interest and pride in James's progress at Westminster School. William Leigh, who as a young man had patiently carried out commissions for his uncle, was still ready to serve him in any way possible, entertaining him at Adlestrop and visiting him at Canons.

Meanwhile at Wanstead, long after work at Canons was completed, Sir Richard Child (now Earl Tylney) had continued to improve the grounds of his house, bringing in Lancelot Brown to direct the construction of an elaborate pattern of artificial lakes and James Rocque, the French cartographer and surveyor, to produce plans for further landscaping that was to turn Wanstead into a small English version of Versailles. But while remaining interested in Child's projects, Chandos no longer had any desire to emulate them; even the discoveries made through the giant telescope at Wanstead left him unmoved. Similarly, he was quite prepared to let his former colleagues in London developments – Bathurst and Burlington for instance – push ahead with architectural innovations and experiments that were a deliberate reaction against the baroque splendours of Canons. In the artistic sphere as elsewhere, Chandos was falling behind current fashion, and although he did employ the currently fashionable Brunetti to complete the decoration of his Cavendish Square house, when asked by a kinsman in 1741 to supply him with a portrait, he instinctively thought of Dahl who had been painting members of his family forty years earlier: or, as an alternative, Jonathan Richardson, only marginally more up to date.

Canons and the life of its household in the 1720's and early 1730's was the embodiment of Chandos's ambitions and fortunes, and proved the grandeur, luxury and efficiency that great wealth could achieve. Its rise in popular estimation resembled the flight of a rocket however, which once having reached its height and spent its brilliance, lost momentum and its power to attract attention, and then sank unnoticed into near oblivion. As long as Chandos was alive, people linked the present with his majestic past, and while no longer inclined to wonder, at least refrained from contempt or pity. Only after his death did his name and fame slip from popular memory as quickly as Canons was stripped of its furnishings and destroyed; and ironically, the chief perpetrator of this was the son of whom Chandos had hoped, and for whom he had done, so much.

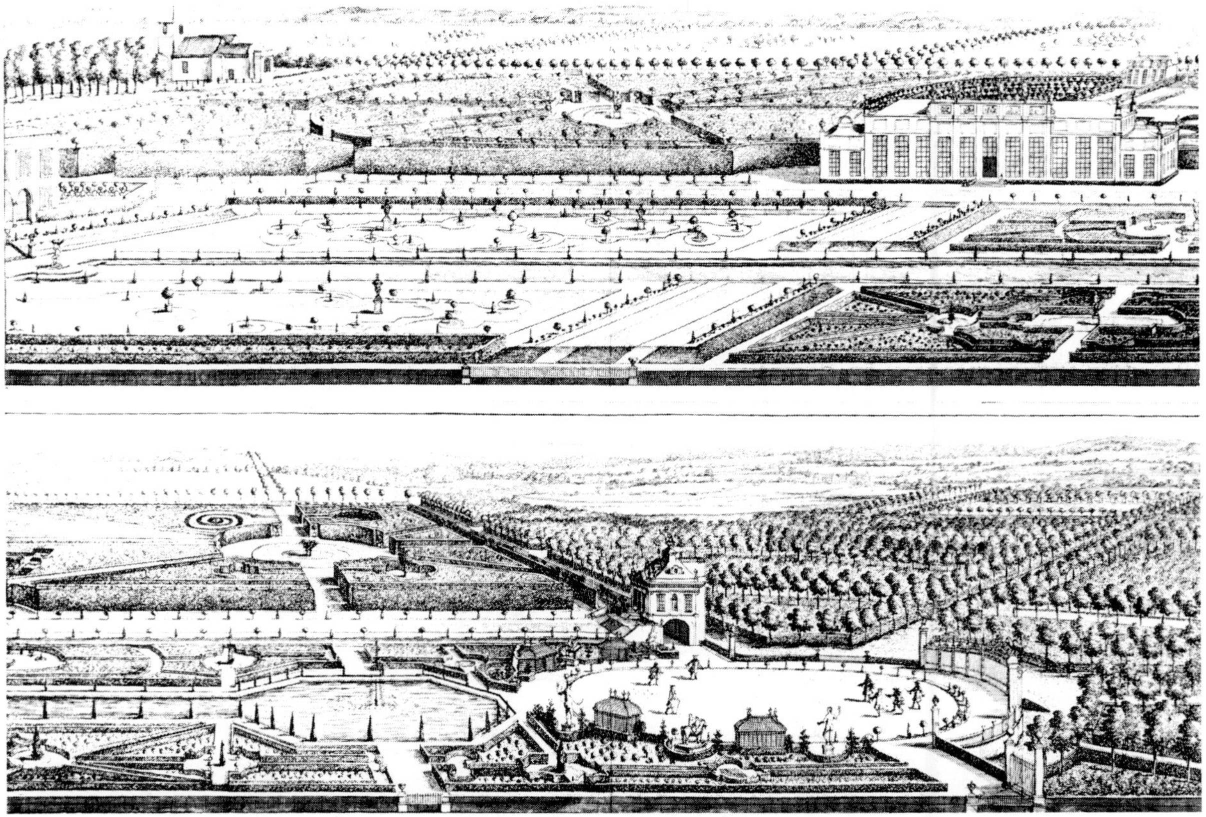

The Grounds of Wanstead House

Epilogue

Chandos died on August 9th 1744 after an illness of a few weeks, possibly aggravated rather than alleviated by the remedies prescribed by his doctors – 'drinks of gill and scurvy grass' and 'salt of wormwood with a little teaspoon of Eaton's styptick'. For several years he had suffered from attacks of asthma, and as he withdrew more from public life, so he took less exercise and noticeably put on weight, until he no longer had the vigorous upright bearing of his middle years. In answer to enquiries about his health, he claimed that he was still fit enough to go out riding as he had in the past, but in fact life was becoming something of a struggle; the heat of summer and the cold of winter seemed equally trying, and at times he felt 'so faint and low-spirited that I am almost weary of life'.

Reactions to the news of the Duke's death were much the same as reactions to his life had been. Some of the public announcements, by their brevity, reflected the lack of interest and respect of those who knew little about him or were critical of him. The *London Post* published a warm appreciation that may well have been contributed by his nephew Dr. Theophilus Leigh since there is a handwritten copy of the passage among the Leigh family papers. This stressed, above all, his *amiable* qualities – sweetness of temper, beneficence and brotherly love. To his wife Lydia, members of his family and of his household, his death was a great loss, not just because it deprived them of a source of material support, but because he had always been ready to offer a sympathetic ear to those in distress and to show an unfailing readiness to put himself at their service. Unlike the *Gentleman's Magazine* which forecast a rosy future for his successor, the family had little faith in Henry, Lord Caernarvon, who now inherited Chandos's title and estates; and events were soon to prove them justified in their views.

In his will Chandos remembered all those who were near and dear to him, as well as faithful servants.[1] His wife, to whom 'next to the great goodness of the Almighty, I owe the greatest comfort I have enjoyed in life' was very well provided for, also his nephews, nieces, grandchildren and godson James Rodney. His servants were to receive a year's wages and money was left for distribution among the poor of Stanmore. Chandos also requested a modest funeral 'with no more pomp nor expense than what mere decency requires and £100 at most will defray'.

Chandos's life had spanned a period of unprecedented changes in political, economic and social spheres, to which he had subscribed unconsciously – going along with the tide of events that disposed of Stuart absolutism and brought in Parliamentary sovereignty, keeping abreast of economic developments, throwing himself wholeheartedly into the role of a patron whose responsibility as well as pleasure it was to employ leading craftsmen and thus commend them to a wider public. While having personal views and scruples, Chandos did not concern himself with philosophical moralising or political and economic theories. He was essentially a realist, living in the present and rather like Walpole whom he admired, he had no lofty ideals that might have made him stand out among his contemporaries. His successes were material ones and his influence limited to his own immediate circle, so that his death caused few ripples beyond that circle.

The fortunes of the Brydges family during the lifetime of Chandos, his son and grandson, proved the belief held by Robert Atkyns the historian, that landed families achieving fame and fortune rarely retained their importance beyond the third generation. In the late 17th century, with an established estate behind him, ambition and a willingness to push himself into public life, a country gentleman might well become prominent and achieve a standard of life commensurate with his status; but as the mid-eighteenth century approached, land ownership and/or public office alone no longer guaranteed success; business acumen and a capacity for manipulating men and circumstances were needed besides, and Chandos had none of the necessary shrewdness, ruthlessness and staying power for this. The results of his undertakings only rarely measured up to the effort he put into them or impressed his contemporaries: although Lord Onslow, more inclined to be censorious than generous in his estimation of the Duke, did acknowledge that

> 'he had parts of understanding and knowledge, experience of men and business, with a sedateness of mind and a gravity of deportment, which more qualified him than what the wisest men have generally been possessed with'.

Alexander Pope, in his *Epistle to Lord Burlington,* which even if not an overt attack on Chandos at least contained some veiled references to him, foretold more truly than he could have known, the fate of Canons.

> Another age shall see the golden ear
> Imbrown the slope and nod on the parterre,
> Deep harvest bury all his pride has plann'd
> And laughing Ceres reassume the land.

Within a short time of Chandos's death, his heir started to realise his father's assets, putting up for auction most of the contents of Canons, the house itself and the Stanmore estate, although Chandos had clearly envisaged these remaining intact, since in his will he left 'to Lord Caernarvon, plate and pictures, books and manuscripts, to go with Canons as heirlooms'. The sale, begun in 1747, was widely advertised in the press and the catalogue drawn up in connection with it is a valuable source of information as to what remained at that point of Chandos's creation, since all the furnishings and decorations were listed room by room and described in some detail. For some reason, the lots were disposed of over a prolonged period and realised a mere fraction (£11,000) of the £200,000 that had originally been spent on the place. William Hallett, the purchaser of the house and grounds, pulled down what remained of the building, and replaced it with a smaller compact dwelling, and proceeded to turn the whole of the grounds to agricultural use.

In the final chapter of the *Life and Circumstances of James Brydges*, Collins Baker tried to trace the whereabouts of some of the outstanding features removed from Canons, but inevitably some of his findings were conjectural and in any case, most of the objects removed from their intended context lost their identity in the process. However, it is certain that the magnificent marble staircase from inside and some of the iron railings from outside the house were bought by the Earl of Chesterfield for his residence in South Audley Street; 'the initials C in the ironwork only needed the replacement of the ducal coronet by an earl's' to make it available' commented Vertue. The columned portico that had graced the entrance to Canons was made into a feature – sadly disproportionate – of Hendon Hall; a pair of gates from one of the lodges in the park was bought for the parish church of St. John's, Hampstead; and some of the garden ornaments appeared in due course at Stowe, Buckinghamshire. But we do have two indusputable reminders of Canons much as they were in Chandos's time. The first is the church of St. Lawrence,

Canons rebuilt by William Hallett

Interior of Great Witley Church

Whitchurch, which still retains its original box pews, the grisaille wall paintings of Francesco Slater, Laguerre's ornate ceiling, and of course the Monument room which commemorates Chandos's connection with the church.[2] The second link with Canons is the parish church of St. Michael and All Angels at Great Witley, Worcestershire, where within the stone framework commissioned from James Gibbs by his father, the second Lord Foley inserted the principal decorative fittings of the chapel acquired at the Canons sale. These included the ceiling paintings by Bellucci, the painted windows made by Joshua Price and the carved case that had contained the organ used by Handel while he was working for Chandos. As at St. Lawrence's the total effect is one of European Baroque splendour, astounding to the visitor who steps through the porch from an English country lane expecting to find himself in a typical English parish church.

The new Duke of Chandos, having rid himself of the burden of Canons, even if not very profitably, proceeded to do the same with Shaw Hall, after the death of his father's third wife Duchess Lydia in 1750. She had removed herself from Canons in 1744 and retired to Shaw Hall to live out her widowhood, choosing also to be buried at Shaw church rather than at Canons, although in his will her husband had expressed a wish that she should be buried alongside him, and 'a marble figure representing the person set up in the Monument room, of the same size and colour with those of my two other wives'. However, even the proceeds of the sale of Canons and Shaw Hall, and the income derived from his father's Hanaper office and estates left in trust for him, were insufficient to keep Henry solvent. Without marked extravagance in any particular direction, but because of sheer improvidence, money ran through his hands like water, and he showed no inclination let alone the determination to get himself out of debt. He was even prepared to suffer the humiliation of having his son petition the King on his behalf, in the hope of securing a sinecure or a pension for him. When his second wife died in 1759, he looked for another and found one in Elizabeth Major, considerably his junior, 'remarkable for a sweetness of temper and a fortune of £30,000,' of which £21,000 was handed over to Henry a fortnight before the wedding to clear his outstanding debts. It is not known whether in the four years of life that remained to him Henry managed to run through the residue of his wife's fortune, but it seems almost inevitable that he did.

In spite of Henry's three marriages and his son Lord Wilton's two, there was no direct male descent from Chandos's immediate family, although Brydges blood was handed down through females in certain families – the Leighs of Adlestrop (and later of Stoneleigh), the Kearneys of Kildare, Ireland, and the Dukes of Buckingham. The link with the Leighs was doubly strong, through the marriage of Chandos's sister Mary with Theophilus Leigh and then of his grand-daughter Caroline with Theophilus's grandson James, and as well as these marriage ties, there seems to have been very real affection between the two families. The connection with the Kearney family was also twofold, since first Chandos's niece Henrietta married John Kearney, and then their son Henry John married Augusta, Chandos's grand-daughter the only child of Caernarvon's second marriage. A connection with Stowe and the Buckingham family was established when Anne Elizabeth, daughter of James Lord Wilton, married the Duke of Buckingham, taking with her the bulk of the family papers, which now constitute the Stowe Collection owned by the Huntington Library in California, whence the greater part of our knowledge of Chandos must be derived, for it consists of 70 books of letters written by and to the Duke, domestic and estate accounts, and bills.

The mass of evidence in the Stowe Collection reflects the weightiness of the business which a person in Chandos's position might be expected to undertake, that is, assuming that he took his reponsibilties as seriously as the latter did. It is immaterial that some of the correspondence was abortive, in so far as it consisted of enquiries and requests that came to naught; it is, in any case, a monument to the Duke's powers of application and the disciplined routine of his days, since wherever he was, the sequence continued. His business letters reveal an attention to detail that was admirable in some respects, though it could lapse into pettiness on occasion; they also reflect his impatience and stubbornness when thwarted in any way, his choler rising in inverse ratio to the significance of the cause of it. For instance, in addition to his dispute with architects over their fees, workmen over ill-fulfilled commissions and tenants over non-payment of rents, there was a two-year-long dispute with a picture-restorer Christopher Cock who was entrusted with the cleaning of the famous Raphael cartoons, and was accused by Chandos of having mutilated them instead. Rather than let Cock get away with his offence, Chandos threatened a lawsuit for damages and conscripted numerous witnesses in his own defence, only to allow the whole matter to lapse in the end and be settled out of court.

Yet there was a reverse side to Chandos's disproportionate obsession with details, that amounted to a virtue. It was his willingness to concern himself with details that led to so many satisfactory marriage settlements being made for nephews, nieces and godchildren: examples of the best workmanship being acquired to adorn Canons: posts and promotions being obtained for servants and dependants: places at Harrow, Charterhouse and Oxford secured and financed, on behalf of relatives and friends. What he deemed worth doing, he did well; and when he was disposed to give he gave generously of his time, money, efforts and magnanimity. The outstanding instance of this was, of course, his reaction to Pope's satirical views expressed in the *Epistle to Lord Burlington*. Possibly it was popular inclination rather than Pope's deliberate intention that the details in the description of Timon's villa should be indentified with the well-publicised features of Canons, but it was a known fact that Pope was no admirer of the Baroque traditions that appealed to Chandos, preferring instead the enthusiasm of Burlington and Bathurst for Classical styles. Nevertheless, when Pope wrote apologetically to Chandos, the latter denied that he had taken any offence over the incident but rather was in sympathy with the poet for having his work thus interpreted:

> I am much troubled to find . . . you are under any uneasiness at the application the town has made of Timon's character in your epistle to the Earl of Burlington. . . . It would indeed be a real concern to me, did I believe one of your judgment had designedly given grounds for their imbibing an opinion so disadvantageous of me. But as your obliging letter is sufficient to free me from this apprehension, I can with great indifference bear the insults they bestow, and not find my self hurt by 'em; nor have I reason to be much disturb'd when I consider how many better persons are the daily objects of their unjust censures.[3]

Necessarily, Chandos's own correspondence and accounts are very much concerned with his public persona. A more intimate picture of his private self emerges from other people's writings. The Tyberton cousins in whose company he spent his early years and who always formed part of his family background, while never on casually intimate terms with him, nevertheless regarded him as a friend. It is clear from their letters that they were always welcome at Canons no matter how many other guests were there, that even on formal occasions Chandos would unbend to them, and that they accepted his ducal role as the inseparable reverse of his kindly cousinship. A visit to Canons enabled them to rub shoulders with the great as well as providing them with a home from home when they were in London; and Chandos's connections with bankers, lawyers and the City were made available to them when they needed credit, a legal matter settled or some business transacted.

Long before she married her cousin James Brydges in 1713, Cassandra Willoughby had started to keep a 'Journal' in which she recorded an account of journeys made with her brother, together with notes of family happenings – mainly births, marriages, illnesses and deaths. These necessarily included references to the Brydges family to which she was already related through her mother's sister, Elizabeth Barnard. After her marriage the entries became briefer as her wifely role began to absorb more and more of her time, but she wrote enough between 1713 and the close of the 'Journal' in 1718 to show how she and her husband were almost constantly together, travelling between Canons and London, visiting friends in the London area, entertaining at Canons and putting in attendance at Court.

> May ye 27 (1716) being Trinity Sunday, the Bishop of Carlisle preached a Sermon at Whitchurch and dined at Canons with several more gentlemen. That evening my Lord and I went to the house in Albemarle Street.
>
> August ye 1st. I went with my Lord to Hampton Court and after being in ye Gallery where was ye King, Prince (of Wales), little Princes and Princesses, dined with ye Dutches of Shrewsbury, ye Lady of ye Bed-Chamber, then in-Waiting. After dinner made a visit to Madam Kilmansach (Kilmansegge).

The partnership was based on true companionship, and if Brydges was a demanding husband at times, Cassandra was assuredly a willingly acquiescent wife. Her letters revealed the regular social calls that were made on their time, the frequent demands on her husband's pocket, the acknowledgment of his many kindnesses. When writing on his behalf, she was content to state his views, and never had any reservations about the correctness of 'Mr. Brydges's' judgment and decisions.

Duchess Cassandra's pleasingly literate hand and style are also evident in *The Register*, started by Chandos's mother and added to by her successive daughters-in-law – Mary Lake, Cassandra and Lydia Davall: also Caernarvon's second wife Anne Jeffries, and briefly by Caernarvon himself on the death of Anne. As well as a record of births, christenings, marriages and burials, it includes testimonials to the character of some of those mentioned, probably honest appraisals since the book was intended for family perusal only, though allowances must be made for motherly pride and wifely devotion. We have already noted Lady Chandos's recommendation of her son as a source of support to the family: she also believed him to be 'a man of singular generosity and compassion to all', and considered that 'he discharg'd his trust (as Paymaster General) with a great deal of honour, honesty and much reputation'. In her tribute, Duchess Lydia wrote of 'his sincere repentance for everything he thought he had err'd in' and expressed the hope that 'if gratitude has not quite forsaken the earth, his forgiving and sincerely religious nature will make his memory dear to everyone that knew him'. Certainly, throughout, *the Register* affords evidence of Chandos's unfailing conscientiousness where family obligations were concerned, and of liberality widely bestowed.

Perhaps those who knew Chandos best, apart from his immediate family, were the Leighs of Adlestrop, whose affection for him did not blind them to his faults and foibles. Chandos's eldest sister Mary, wife of Theophilus Leigh, most resembled her mother whose judgement the family respected, and her very high regard for the family she married into was equalled by theirs for the Brydges. It is among the Leigh family papers that the earliest of Chandos's letters can be found, one of congratulation to Theophilus and Mary on their marriage, accompanied by a poem in pastoral style, not a literary masterpiece by any means, but clearly a token of sincere goodwill. Neither politically nor commercially as committed as the Brydges, the Leighs were nevertheless prominent in Gloucestershire affairs and owned property in London as well, so they had a certain status in both places. Theophilus was not prepared to go as far as Lady Chandos in believing her son completely guiltless where his conduct in public office was concerned, but as a man of the world, capable of keeping things in proportion, he considered his brother-in-law a very minor transgressor as compared with others, and certainly not deserving of public censure or disgrace.

Letters exchanged between Theophilus and his son William at the time of James Brydges's second marriage, showed an amused tolerance of their kinsman's secrecy over the whole affair (which seems to have been public property anyway) but always on Theophilus's side there was a desire that William should show no disrespect for, or impatience with his uncle, but a willingness to serve him, even though sometimes the fulfilment of commissions did not give satisfaction. The attitude of Brydges to his nephew was that of a father to his son: and after Theophilus's death the bond was strengthened so that during his last years William Leigh was one of the people the Duke turned to and confided in most often. Had he known of it, nothing would have pleased the latter more than the marriage that was to take place in due course between his grand-daughter Caroline and William's son James. The private letters exchanged between the Brydges and the Leighs expressing congratulations on births and marriages, concern over illnesses and sympathy in bereavements, were spontaneous and unaffected. In such instances at any rate, familiarity bred not contempt but respect and genuine consideration.

Ambition drove Chandos into place-seeking and social climbing: conscientiousness and pride then obliged him to take his various roles seriously and to fill them to the best of his ability. This effort stretched his resources – of wealth, energy and character – to the utmost, and the nervous tension that drove him into frenzied activity as a young man, developed into considerable strain later on, for he was never completely sure of himself and therefore dared not relax or take himself less than very seriously. Rarely did he show a sense of humour which might have helped him to keep things in proportion and to establish priorities, so that instead of giving equal attention to both weighty and inconsequential matters he could have allowed the latter to drop altogether. In a less important position, his capacity for taking pains and indisputable good will, would have earned him an immediate and lasting reputation; as it was, his prominent role and his interpretation of it, demanded qualities of daring, ingenuity and panache which were foreign to his nature, so that the performance was not as convincing as it should have been.

The tribute to Chandos in the *London Post* would make a neat and fitting conclusion to this study; as would the epitaph on his tomb at St. Lawrence, Whitchurch, but these were written for public perusal and in the conventional idiom required for such passages. So perhaps more telling is a comment on Canons and its creator written by the Rev. Stebbing Shaw in 1788, over forty years after Chandos's death, with no possible ulterior motive in mind:

> Near Edgware is Canons, once celebrated and still remembered for the magnificent seat built here by the splendid Duke of Chandos who lived in a style and exercised an hospitality that almost eclipsed royalty itself. Munificence rather than vanity seems to have prompted his expenses. He was the patron of literature and the arts and possessed a most generous and feeling heart.

St Lawrence's Church, Whitchurch

Obituary

ON THE DUKE OF CHANDOS

And is he gone? The gentlest, noblest mind,
The lover and the love of human kind.
Chandos whose wealth by every virtue glac'd,
Showed how Heavens' bounty shines when justly placed.
So true a judge, a patron to direct,
A hand so generous, so true a heart.
All who could feel its warmth, his power confessed,
And all who felt it, own such greatness blessed.
Now let the Muse, who feels his absense most
Deplore his virtues or example lost.

The Gentleman's Magazine, August 1744

Notes on the Text

Abbreviations:

B.M.   British Museum
H.M.C.   Historical Manuscripts Commission
H.R.O.   Hereford Record Office
O.R.O.   Oxford Record Office
S.B.T.   Shakespeare Birthplace Trust, Stratford upon Avon
S.T.   Huntington Library: Stowe MSS.

All quotations from Duchess Cassandra's writings, as indicated in the text, are from her Letter Books and Journal SBT. Gloucestershire Papers DR20.

Chapter 1

1. Dewsall, Aconbury and Wilton Castle were all situated a few miles to the west of Ross and near to the main Hereford–Ross road. Dewsall, an Elizabethan manor-house, with panelled rooms and richly carved fireplaces and stairway, is now in a dilapidated state; Aconbury and Wilton Castle have disappeared.
2. Sudeley Castle. At the end of the Civil Wars, this was slighted and made uninhabitable, and ultimately passed out of the ownership of the Brydges family.
3. His connections with the City, through the Turkey Company, made him suspect in the eyes of the King who was aware that the London merchants were supporting the Whig opponents of the monarchy.
4. S.B.T. Gloucestershire Papers DR20 Box 18.
5. Quoted in the *Gentleman's Magazine* LXII (1792) Dr Knipe was to succeed Dr Busby as Headmaster of Westminster a few years later.
6. At the time, the completed Quadrangle was likened to Versailles. The finishing touch to its appearance was a wrought iron screen with gates to the garden, the work of Thomas Robinson, a pupil of Tijou. The Chandos arms which adorned the gates have now disappeared.
7. Macky, John. *A Journey through England.*
8. *Huntington Library Quarterly*, No. VIII (1944).

Chapter 2

1. At this point, Lord and Lady Chandos were living in the Deanery, while James on his visits to Hereford, had a house in St Owen's Street, now destroyed.
2. Marlborough. *Correspondence of the Duchess of Marlborough.* The ring consisted of a cameo of Marlborough covered by a diamond cut as thin as a piece of glass.

183

3. *Victoria County History of Herefordshire*, Vol. II.
4. *Huntington Library Quarterly* No. III (1939–40).
5. Quoted in Beattie, J.M. *The English Court under George I*.
6. *Ibid.*

Chapter 3

1. B.M. Sloane MSS 4046.
2. Bolitho, Hector, *The Drummonds of Charing Cross*.
3. S.T. 58 Vol. 5, May 1710.
4. H.M.C. *Portland V*, Harley Correspondence.
5. H.R.O. A81/IV
6. *Ibid.*
7. Johnson, Joan, *Excellent Cassandra*, p. 96.

Chapter 4

1. Macky, John, *A Journey through England*.
2. H.M.C. *Portland V*, Harley Correspondence.
3. A strict hierarchical order was observed in the Dining-Room at Canons, in respect of tables and those who sat at them – the Chaplain's table coming below that of the Duke, the Officers of the Household below the Gentlemen of the House and so on. The domestic and outdoor staff conformed to a similar order in the Servants' Hall.
4. Johnson, Joan, *Excellent Cassandra*, p. 44.
5. Gildon, Charles, *The Vision*, quoted in above.
6. H.R.O. A81/IV.

Chapter 5

1. S.B.T. Gloucestershire Papers, DR20 Box 18.
2. H.R.O. A81/IV.
3. *Ibid.*
4. S.B.T. DR20 Box 18.
5. Some of Emma's troubles are discussed in *Excellent Cassandra* P. 104.
6. S.T, 57. Letters to Katherine Bourchier, Sept. 1716 to Sept. 1717.
7. *Ibid.*
8. *Ibid.*
9. S.T. 57, November 1717.
10. H.R.O. A81/IV, Letter-senders were those who broke the law of 1723 which made it a felony for anyone to send letters anonymously or signed with a fictitious name, demanding money or threatening harm to persons or property.

Chapter 6

1. S.T. 57, Vol. 39, p. 231.
2. S.B.T. DR20, Box 18.
3. S.T. 57, Vol. 47, p. 172.
4. S.B.T. DR20 Box 18.
5. S.T. 57 Vol. 43.

Notes   185

Chapter 7

1. Quoted in Sprague-Allen, A. *Tides in English Taste*.
2. O.R.O. Dil I/p/1a.
3. O.R.O. Dil I/p/3b.
4. Plans of the lay-out of the rooms at Canons are given in Baker, H.M. Colins, *Life and Circumstance of James Brydges*, at pp. 128 and 144.
5. Details of the Canons 'Musick' are given in *Excellent Cassandra*, Appendix IV.
6. Rudder, S., *Gloucestershire*.

Chapter 8

1. ST 57 Vol. 32 p. 210. Letter to Mr Farquarson.
2. ST 57 Vol. 47. Letter to Henry Perrot.
3. ST 57 Vol. 32. Letter to Mr Ferguson.
4. ST 57 Vol. 32.

Chapter 9

1. S.T. 57. Vol. 46, September 1735.
2. A rare instance of Caernarvon's concern for his children and an unexpected sensitivity occurs in a letter written to their nurse when Lord Wilton was recovering from small-pox. Caernarvon asked that 'when Lord Wilton is able to rise, you will take great care he does not catch cold . . . and that you will not suffer him to look in a glass for fear he should be startled, since when he first gets his wig, he will want to see for himself' S.B.T. DR20, Box 18.
3. S.T. 57, Vol. 39, p. 231.

Epilogue

1. The terms of the will are quoted in full in Baker, pp. 465–468.
2. Recently, the ceilings and wall paintings in the church were found to be in a parlous state, and an appeal was launched to finance their restoration. A team of two German and two English restorers (specialists in Baroque painting) were commissioned to carry out this work, which has involved an analysis of the original colours and plaster used, as well as meticulous re-painting.
3. Quoted in Baker, p. 434.

Bibliography

Manuscript Sources

Brydges Correspondence	Herefordshire County Record Office A81/IV.
Chamberlayne MSS	Gloucestershire County Record Office D621.
Leigh MSS	Gloucestershire County Record Office D612.
Dillon Archives	Oxfordshire County Record Office Dil.I.
Sloane MSS	British Museum 4046.
Stoneleigh MSS	Shakespeare Birthplace Trust Glos. Papers DR20, Box 18.
Stowe MSS	Huntington Library, San Marino, California.
Willoughby, Cassandra	Letter book owned by the North London Collegiate School. Letter book & Journal in Glos. Papers DR20, Box 18.

Contemporary Writings

Addison, Joseph	The Spectator.
Bodleian MSS	Catalogue of Auction at Canons (1747).
Defoe, Daniel	Tour through the Islands of Great Britain.
Gildon, Charles	The Vision (1718).
Humphreys, Samuel	Canons (1728).
Macky, John	A Journey through England (1723).
Pope, Alexander	Collected Works.
Vertue, George	Notebooks. Walpole Society XXIV.

Secondary Sources

Baker, H.M. Collins	Life & Circumstances of James Brydges (1949).
Beard, Geoffrey	Craftsmen & Interior Decoration in England (1981).
Beattie, J.M.	The English Court under George I (1967).
Colvin, H.M.	Biographical Dictionary of English Architects (1954).

Bibliography

Foss, Michael	The Age of Patronage: 1660–1750 (1971).
Genealogist's Magazine	Volume X. The Chandos Register.
Girouard, Mark	Social Life in the English Country House (1978).
Green, David	Henry Wise: Gardener to Queen Anne (1956).
Hook, Judith	The Baroque Age in England (1976).
Johnson, Joan	Excellent Cassandra. The Life and Times of the Duchess of Chandos (1982).
Lees-Milne, James	Earls of Creation (1962).
	English Country Houses 1688–1715 (1970).
Moir, Esther	The Discovery of Britain: the English Tourists (1964).
Osborne, H.	The Oxford Companion to Art (1970).
Plumb, J.H.	The First Four Georges (1956).
Rudé, J.	Hanoverian London (1976).
Sprague-Allen, A.	Tides in English Taste 1619–1800 (1969).
Summerson, Sir John	Architecture in Britain 1530–1830 (1953).
	Classical Houses in the 18th century (1959).
	Georgian London (1962).
Waterhouse, Ellis	Painting in Britain 1530–1790 (1979).
Wilson, Charles	England's Apprenticeship (1965).

Acknowledgements

Since I have drawn to a considerable extent on the Chandos papers in the Huntington Library, San Marino, I must primarily thank Miss Mary Robertson Keeper of Manuscripts there, for despatching material for me to study: and the Librarian for graciously allowing me to quote from this. Extracts from Cassandra's Letter Book have been quoted with the kind permission of the Governors of the North London Collegiate School.

I am also indebted to the staffs of the Record Offices at Hereford, Gloucester and Stratford upon Avon: and of the Bodleian Library and the Ashmolean Museum for their interest and help when I have been working there.

Through conversation and correspondence a number of queries have been resolved by staff at the Guildhall Museum, the Courtauld Institute and the Newbury Museum: by Lady Patricia Phipps and Mr David Verey. Mr Anthony Kersting has been most helpful in the search for illustrations. Material on Wanstead was patiently researched by Mr and Mrs F Johnson; and up-to-date information on St Lawrence's Church, Whitchurch, came from the Friends of St Lawrence.

My thanks are also due to Dr Margaret Toynbee for her unfailing encouragement and support: to Miss Sybil Harris for typing the manuscript: and to Alan Sutton and his staff for their help through all the stages of production.

For their kind permission to reproduce plates, I am greatly indebted to Lord Middleton, Mr Anthony Kersting, the Courtauld Institute, the Ashmolean Museum, the National Portrait Gallery, the British Library, the Newbury Museum, the Yale Centre for British Art and Country Life Magazine; and to other owners who wish to remain anonymous.

Index

Illustrations are given in *italic*.

Adlestrop 21, 88, 114, 116, 157, 176
Ailesbury, Earl of 84
Allen, Ralph *123*, *124*, 125
Anne, Princess and Queen 10, 32, 35–36, 45, 120
Archer, Thomas 121, 125, 127
Artari, Giovanni 129–130
Atkyns, Annabella 87, 93
   Elizabeth see Walter
   Sir Robert 171

Bagutti, Giovanni 129
BARNARD, Elizabeth see Chandos
   Emma see Child
   Sir Henry 10, 15, 17, 53
Barnsley (Glos) 129, 142
BATH 106, 108, 111, 112, *113*, 115, 144, 150
Bathurst, Lord 78, 81, 115, 120, 122, 126, 144, 148
Bellucci, Antonio 130, 137, 138, 175
Bernstorff, Baron 47
Bingley, Robert Lord 78, 81, 115, 120–121, 125, 126
Blathwayt, William, 122, 127, 148
Blenheim 122, 146, 150
Bolingbroke, Henry St John, Viscount 36, *37*, 40, 42, 45
Bothmer, Baron 45, 47
BOURCHIER, Brereton *90*, 91, 142
   Katherine 66, 91–92, 140
   Martha see Perrot
Bridgwater (Somerset) 105, 129
Brunetti, Gaetano 157, 168
BRYDGES,
   Anne see Walcot

Caroline Lady 88, 161, 167
Catherine Lady 83, 161, *163*
Elizabeth see Dawson
Elizabeth see Walter
Francis (of Tyberton) 64, 66, 73
Henry Dr 18, 62, 87
James, 8th Baron see Chandos
James, 1st Duke see Chandos
James see Wilton
Jane, Lady 84, 87, 161–2, *163*
Mary see Leigh
William (of Tyberton) 61, 75
Burlington, Lord 78, 81, 115, 121, 126, 144
Busby, Dr Richard *19*, 21–22

Cadogan, Lord 40
CAERNARVON, Catherine Marchioness of 83, 161–162
   Henry, Earl of 82, 84, 86, 118, 158, 172, 175, 186
   John, Earl of *27*, 82–83
   Mary, Marchioness of 84, 118, 161
Campbell, Colen 81, 116, 120, 126, 138
CANONS 11, 62, 64–65, 71–72, 74–75, 77, 136–139, 145–146, 148–154, *151*, *152*, 167, *173*, 178, 180, 184
Castlemain, see Child
Cavendish Square 70–71, 78, 122, 158, 168
Chamberlayne, Edmund 72, 91, 114
   Emma 91, 93, 114, 185
CHANDOS, Anne Duchess of: *160*, 161, 178
   Cassandra Duchess of: 10, 21, 51, 54, 60, 62, *63*, 64, 66–67, 77, 82, 84, 93–94, 106, 145, 147, 155–157, 162, 178
   Elizabeth Lady 10, 14–15, 21, 178

Henry, 2nd Duke see Caernarvon
James, 8th Lord 14, 17, 18, 32, 53
JAMES 1st DUKE *2, 50*
   benefactions 95, 96, 98, 165, 167, 177
   character 10–14, 18, 67, 95, 126, 166, 170, 176–177, 179–180
   early career 10, 15, 18, 22, 25–26, 28, 31
   family concern 14, 87–88, 91
   health 66, 157, 162, 165, 170
   homes 61–62, 64–65, 68, 70
   marriages 12, 28, 62, 157–158
   Member of Parliament 32–33, 35, 36, 39
   official appointments 33, 48, 101–102, 165
   Paymaster General 35, 39–40, 45
   speculations 57–58, 60, 102, 104–105, 108, 155
   will 170–171
   Lydia Duchess of: 106, 157, *159*, 175, 178–179
Charlton, Sir Job 15, 17
CHILD, Emma Lady 10, 15
   Sir Josiah 10, 21, 54, *55*, 57, 62, 144
   Sir Richard 21, 64, 78, 93–94, 116, 126, 136, 144, 148, 168
Coffee-houses 11, 26, 53

Dahl, Michael *2*, 12, *50*, 168
Danvers, Beata 36, 42
Davall, see Chandos, Lydia Duchess of
Dawson, Elizabeth 10, 21, 26, 91, 92
Defoe, Daniel 119, 139, 150
Dewsall (Hereford) 15, 18, 184
Ditchley (Oxon) 112, 122, 126–127, 130, *131*, *132*, 147–148
Drummond, Andrew 58, *59*, 185
   John 58, 60, 133
Dyrham (Glos) 122, *128*, 148
Dysart, Countess of 83, 161

East India Company 10, 54
Enfield Chace 102
Estate management 15–17, 71, 105, 140–154

Gardens 114, 115, 144–147
George I 32, 45, 47, 48, 51, 76, 120
   II 51, 120

Prince of Denmark 33, *34*
Gibbons, Grinling 133, *134*, 138, 157
Gibbs, James 121–122, 127, 157, 175
Gildon, Charles 72–73, 119
Godolphin, Sidney Lord 36, 41, 47
Golden Square *30*, 31, 61

Hallett, William 154, 172
Handel, George Frederick 75, 76, 96, *97* 137
Hanover 10, 25–26, 51, 83
Harley, Edward 70, 78
Hauderoy, Samuel 127
Hereford 26, 32, 39, 84, 86
Highmore, Joseph *160*
Holloway, Benjamin 105, 129
Hore, John 106
Hoskyns, Sir Hungerford 88
   Rev. J. 88
Hudson, Thomas 27, *97*, 136, *159*
Hulsbergh, H *23*, 139
Huntington Library 176

Inwood, Colonel 87, 93, 118, 161

Jacob, Alexander (Junior) 91, 92, 93
   Alexander (Senior) 53, 91–92
   Elizabeth see Dawson
James II 18, 32
James, John 122, 138
Jefferies, Anne see Chandos, Duchess of

Kearney, John 87, 176
Kent, William 126–127, 130, 150
Kentchurch (Hereford) 15, 114
Kielmansegge, Mme 47
Kneller, Sir Godfrey *38*, 44, 46, 130, 136

Laguerre, Louis 130, 138, 175
Lake, Sir Thomas 28, 62
   Mary *27*, 28, 31, 62, 65, 157, 178
Leers, Renier 25, 135
LEIGH, James 88
   Mary 88, *89*, 111, 116
   Theophilus 16, 18, 42, 66, 84, 88, 179
   Dr Theophilus 88, 91, 114, 161, 170
   William 14, 62, 76, 135, 146, 157, 167–168, 179

Index

Lichfield, Lord 112, 122, 126–127, 144
London, George 144, 146, 148
LONDON 9, 26, 28, 53, 68, 73–74, 99–100, 112, 129, 141, 143, 150

Macky, John 48, 111, 119, 133, 150
Marlborough, John Churchill, Duke of 35, 40, 42, *43*, 47
    Sarah, Duchess of 35–36, *44*, 48, 78, 184
Marylebone 70, 77
Masham, Abigail 41, 42
Middleton see Willoughby Thomas
Montigny, John 135

New River Company 102
Nollekens, Joseph *80*, 136
Nost, Jan van 133, 150

Opera 76–77
Oxford Balliol College 82
    New College 22, *23*, *24*, 184
Oxford, Robert Harley, Earl of 36, 39, 41–42, *46*, 70

Pepusch, Dr John 75, 96, 165
PERROT, Henry 93, 115, 118, 129, 142, 144, 148, 157, 165
    Martha 92–93, 158
Pope, Alexander 13, 81, 115, 172, 177
Price, John 125, 127

Ranelagh Gardens 77, *79*
Red Lion Square 26, *29*, 61
Richardson, Jonathan *37*, 136, 168
Robethon, Jean 47
Rodney, James 165, 171
Royal African Company 57–58, 72
Royal Office of Works 121–122
Royal Society 25, 122, 141

St James's Palace 48, *49*, 50–51
    Park *49*, 77
    Square 31, 68, *69*, 70, 71, 73
    Church, Picadilly 31, 68
St Lawrence's, Whitchurch 11, 31, 74, 130, 138, 150, 161, 172, 175, 180, *181*, 186
Schulenberg, Mme 47
Serena, Francesco 129–130

Shaw Hall, Newbury 106, *107*, 112, 129, 145, 147, 156, 158, 167, 175
Shepherd, Edward 105, 106, 125
Shrewsbury, Lord 78, 122, 125
Sion Hill, Isleworth 62
Slater, Francesco 138, 175
Sloane, Sir Hans *56*, 57–58
Smith, Francis 129
South Sea Company 60–61
Spanish Succession, War of 35–36, 40, 45, 53
Strong, Edward 127
Sudeley Castle (Glos) 17, 184
Sun Fire Insurance Company 88, 102
Switzer, Stephen 81, 144

Talman, William 122, 148
Theatres 76, 77
Thornhill, Sir James 130
Tijou, Jean 133, 184
Tollemache, Catherine see Caernarvon
Tunbridge Wells 66, 73, 108, *109*, *110*, 111
Turkey Company 17, 53–54

Vanbrugh, Sir John 121–122

Walcot, Anne 21, 91
Walpole, Sir Robert *38*, 47, 60, 78, 119, 165–166
Walter, Lady Elizabeth 87
    Sir Robert 87, 114
Wanstead (Essex) *80*, 116, *117*, 126, 138, 148, 150, 168
Westminster School 21–22, 65, 167
William III 10, 22, 32, 146
WILLOUGHBY
    Cassandra see Chandos, Duchess of
    Francis 15, 25, 144
    Thomas 64–65
Wilton, Lord 84, 118, 161–162, *164*, 167
Wise, Henry 144, 146
Witley (Worcs) 144, 146, *174*
Wood, John 108, 125

York Buildings and Water Company 71, 102, *103*

Zoffany, Johan *59*, 136